PELICAN BOOKS

A 261

A FORGOTTEN KINGDOM

SIR LEONARD WOOLLEY

A FORGOTTEN KINGDOM

BEING A RECORD OF THE RESULTS OBTAINED
FROM THE EXCAVATION OF TWO MOUNDS,
ATCHANA AND AL MINA,
IN THE TURKISH HATAY

BY

SIR LEONARD WOOLLEY

*

PENGUIN BOOKS
MELBOURNE · LONDON · BALTIMORE

Penguin Books Ltd, Harmondsworth, Middlesex

U.S.A.: Penguin Books Inc., 3300 Clipper Mill Road, Baltimore 11, Md
[*Educational Representative:*
D. C. Heath & Co, 285 Columbus Avenue, Boston 16, Mass]

AUSTRALIA: Penguin Books Pty Ltd, 200 Normanby Road
Melbourne, S.C.5, Victoria

AGENT IN CANADA: Riverside Books Ltd, 47 Green Street
Saint Lambert, Montreal, P.Q.

—

Made and printed in Great Britain by
Hunt, Barnard and Co Ltd, Aylesbury, Bucks
Collogravure Plates by
Harrison and Sons Ltd

—

First published 1953

Contents

List of Plates

List of Text Figures

LIST OF TEXT FIGURES

Most of the text figures were drawn by
Miss Freda Hands

Editorial Foreword

BY

M. E. L. MALLOWAN

Professor of Western Asiatic Archaeology, University of London

THE narrative of *A Forgotten Kingdom* takes the reader on a journey of adventure through more than four thousand years of man's progress in a corner of NW. Syria. Here we may see what the spade can do to extract knowledge from the ground and how a judicious choice of ancient sites can restore to the light long forgotten sequences of civilization.

Sir Leonard Woolley with his customary skill and imagination guides us through the territory which he has investigated; he interprets for us when the archaeology is difficult to follow and seeks for meaning where the material appears to be obscure. Many problems remain to be resolved, but happily there is more evidence yet to come. The reader who wishes to go even more deeply into the ancient literary sources from Alalakh is recommended to read a forthcoming work by Mr D. J. Wiseman entitled 'The Alalakh Tablets' (*Occasional Publications of the British Institute at Ankara No.* 2), in which he has translated many texts which throw further light on life within the city between about 1800 and 1400 B.C. Over a still wider tract of territory Dr O. R. Gurney's Pelican Book on *The Hittites* has already told us what is known about another Kingdom which was often in close touch with that which is now described.

*

Professor Mallowan is the general editor of the Pelican Series of Near Eastern and Western Asiatic archaeologies.

To

MAJOR-GENERAL SIR NEILL MALCOLM
K.C.B.

*but for whom there would have been no
digging at Atchana*

*

Introduction

THE excavation of the two sites, al Mina and Atchana, in the Turkish Hatay, was carried on for a total of seven spring or autumn seasons between 1936 and 1949. Since a considerable part of the expense was met by public funds it would in any case be only fair that the results of more general interest should be rendered to the public, but in writing this book I have had in mind something other than that duty.

Before we began work nothing at all was known about either of the mounds; there was nothing to connect them with any place or event in ancient history. As the work went on we were able to argue that al Mina must be identified with a harbour mentioned indeed by several classical writers under the name Posideium, but so casually mentioned that even its position on the coast remained conjectural; written documents which we unearthed proved that Atchana was a town named Alalakh, but in all the records of the past that we possess only a single occurrence of that name had been detected. That does not sound very promising. It might well be thought that even if a certain amount of history could be recovered from the ruins of an insignificant town it would be of a purely local character, contributing nothing to our knowledge of civilization's progress, and that money and labour would have been better spent on one of the great centres in which civilization developed.

It is perfectly true that if your object is to illustrate the art of any one country and to recover its national records the proper place to look is the capital of the country or one of its principal cities where artists would have received most patronage and where the archives of administrative offices or of temples would have been kept. Already a great deal of work has been done on such sites with the result that a great deal is now known about most of the ancient states of the Middle East. But that knowledge tends to be self-contained. It was absolutely necessary to begin by gathering material from which the culture of each individual state at different stages of its history could be more or less defined, but the time comes – and has come now – when what we want to know is the history of civilization generally, and for that we have to study the inter-relations between the individual states. The art of any one country will often lead us to suspect the influence of another, but history requires a firmer basis than suspicion, and although the results of international relations may seem fairly obvious we cannot be sure that the apparent debt is a real one nor, if it be real, how or why it was incurred; and if the contact was, as often was the case, indirect, then it is still more difficult to trace it. One of the urgent duties of the archaeologist to-day is to trace those connexions, and he will discover them by digging not at one terminus or the other but on the lines of communication. How to decide on the right line and the right point on the line is a matter partly of geography, partly of history so far as we know it, and altogether (since he is dealing with the unknown) of reasonable probability. Thus in the present case, where the object in view was to trace connexions between the Middle East – Mesopotamia and Anatolia and Lake Van included – and the Aegean, the overland trade routes from the East led us to the extreme north of Syria, and the oversea route demanded a harbour provided with a comparatively easy pass through the mountains to the interior, which led us to al Mina. Since on the coast there was no room for a city important enough to control the mountain passage the pass, and the port, must have been controlled by a town inland. This took us to the Amq plain. Since the plain lay outside the sphere of Egyptian control and before the fourteenth century B.C. was not under the Hittite power centred in

Anatolia it was presumably the site of an independent kingdom which must necessarily have played the part of a buffer state and would therefore, in all probability, illustrate the passage of influences between its more powerful neighbours. The only problem then was to decide which of the many scores of mounds in the plain represented the royal town, since that would, of course, give us the best results for our study.

This was our justification for choosing a historically unknown site on which to dig. We did recover a continuous and fairly detailed history of the town called Alalakh, but my report will, I hope, make it clear that the record possesses much more than local interest. It involves continual reference to the great empires of ancient Sumer, of Babylon, and of Egypt, to the Hittite empire centred on Bogazköy in Anatolia and to the less-known powers of Hurri and Mitanni; it bears on the development of that Cretan art which astonishes us in the palace of Minos at Knossos, it is associated with the Bronze Age culture of Cyprus, bears witness to the eastward expansion of the trade of the Greek islands in the proto-historic age, throws an entirely new light on the economic aspects of the Athenian empire and even, at the last, suggests a Syrian contribution to the Italian Renaissance. This is the outcome of seven seasons of excavation. The book that follows is by way of being an *apologia*. I have tried to prove that to-day, when the cost of foreign excavation has increased ten-fold, when it might be thought that all the best sites, those of the most famous cities of the past, had already been exploited and perhaps exhausted and when therefore the public might excusably turn a deaf ear to the horseleech demands of the field archaeologist, there is yet a vast amount of digging to be done whose results will not merely intrigue the specialist but will open before the eyes of all of us new windows on our common past.

The full and detailed account of our field-work at Atchana is given in *Alalakh*, a volume published by the

Society of Antiquaries of London; that contains the archaeological basis for the conclusions I here put forward, and to it the student who wishes to verify those conclusions must be referred. In this book I have left out, so far as is possible, that raw material which is the special concern of the scholar and have tried to confine myself to what I believe to be of general interest. History should appeal to everyone, but not everyone can be expected to digest the dry-as-dust facts of archaeology; and yet the two things are interdependent. Our knowledge of the ancient world, which is well worth while, cannot advance unless the field archaeologist is enabled to carry on the research from which history is evolved.

The Idri-mi inscription is published by Professor Sidney Smith and the cuneiform tablets by Mr. D. J. Wiseman in *Occasional Publications of the British Institute of Archaeology in Ankara*, Nos. 1 and 2 respectively.

CHAPTER I

The Site

*

In the extreme NW. of Syria, occupying the greater part of the Turkish province of the Hatay, lies the Amq plain. It is a wide and flat alluvial area measuring about thirty miles in either direction, separated only by a line of low hills from the great plateau which stretches past Aleppo to the river Euphrates; on the south it is bounded by a tangle of broken hills, on the west by the lofty range of the Amanus mountains whose further flanks drop precipitously to the Mediterranean, and on the north by the snow-clad peaks of Anti-Taurus. From the east the little river Afrin and from the north the Kara-Su run into the plain and help to fill the marshes and the lake that form its centre; from the south the river Orontes, whose source is in the southern Lebanon, flows through an amazingly tortuous channel and turning westwards at what since Crusading times at least has been called the 'Iron Bridge' enters the valley in which the followers of Alexander built the famous city of Antioch, and then, bursting through the chain of the Amanus, wanders again across the alluvial plain of its own making to the sea.

In modern times the population of this really fertile plain has been but small, for the Amq had, and deserved, the evil reputation of being the most malarial district of Syria; it was scarcely an exaggeration to say that the clouds of mosquitos which at sunset rose from the marshland hid the sky. But that was not always so, and the lake is itself but a

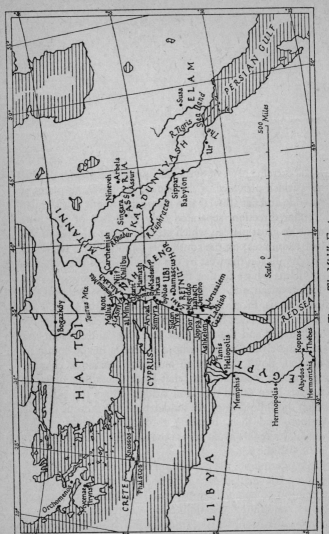

Fig. 1. *The Middle East*

modern feature. To-day, when the drainage works of the Turkish Government have lowered its level, you can lean over the gunwale of your boat and peering down into the clear water see below you the ruins of houses and churches which were built when Antioch was one of the great centres of Christendom; so recently has the change come about. It seems that when in the sixth century A.D. an earthquake destroyed Antioch it also dislodged a vast mass of rock in the side of the ravine half-way between the city and the sea, through which the Orontes runs, and dammed the whole outlet of the three rivers which met in the Amq plain; the entire plain therefore was turned into a stagnant lake whose bed was ever being raised by the silt of the three streams until at last the floods overtopped or broke through the barrage, and the Orontes, wearing for itself a new channel through the built-up mud-flats, could once more reach the sea. But by then the riverside buildings of Roman Antioch were buried beneath thirty feet of mud and the barrier was too high for effective drainage; in the Amq plain the rivers Afrin and Kara-Su came to an inglorious end in marsh and lake.

In antiquity then there was no lake; the plain was well watered but not waterlogged; it was healthy, the summer heats being relieved by the prevailing NW. wind that blew from the snow peaks of Taurus, and its soil was very fertile; it was a desirable land. And that in more ways than one. The barren scrub-speckled slopes of the Amanus mountains were then densely forested with cedar and other hard-wood trees, one of the most precious commodities of the old world; a tributary stream that joined the Orontes below Antioch ran through gravel beds rich in alluvial gold; there was copper ore in the hills facing the sea south of the river's mouth; and if here there were the raw materials for trade the Amq plain by its position made their exploitation easy. This self-contained hollow land was, from the point of view of commerce, the meeting-place of the Great Powers. One could go northwards up the Kara-Su valley to

Marash and the Hittite country; eastwards, only forty miles away across open country, lay Aleppo, and thence the roads led by the Euphrates to Babylon or, crossing the great river at Carchemish, to Nineveh and Asshur, or again, by a NE. branch, to Lake Van and the land of the first workers of iron. Southwards from the plain the caravan-routes passed through Syria by way of Hama (or Hamath) and Homs and so to Damascus or across the length of Palestine to Egypt. Last but not least important was the way of the sea. An easy pass along the Orontes valley led through the mountains to the shore of the Mediterranean where the river's winding mouth made one of the few harbours on this rocky and inhospitable coast, a sheltered roadstead amply sufficient for the little ships of the ancient world; further to the north the less easy but better-known Beilan Pass brings one to the great land-locked Gulf of Alexandretta where again there is good anchorage for ships and in addition a track skirting the sea northwards whereby one can reach the wide and fertile plain of Cilicia.

So favoured a district was certain to attract settlers, and it is not surprising to find that the Amq plain is littered with mounds, something like two hundred in number, each of which represents an ancient town or village or military fortress; they are not all of one date, but all are early and very many of them, as is proved by the potsherds lying on their surface, go back to prehistoric times, even to the Stone Age; from the beginning it was a densely populated area.

The great number of these mounds was embarrassing to the would-be excavator; which of them all was likely to give the best results if our object was to trace the history of the Amq and, in particular, its international trade relations? With the later historical periods we were not concerned, for not only was a good deal known about them but the cultural exchanges which influenced the development of Near Eastern civilization must have taken place early, if at all, and what happened after about 1200 B.C. really lay out-

side the scope of our immediate interest. I could rule out
therefore any mound that had been occupied in Roman or
Islamic days, where the clearing of the top hamper would
mean unremunerative labour and expense, and since we
wanted cultural evidence could reject also any *tell* whose
shape suggested a fortress rather than a residential site; but

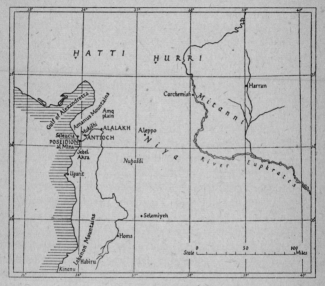

Fig. 2. *The Kingdom and its Neighbours*

even so the choice was uncomfortably wide. Atchana, the
'Thirsty Mound', was selected because it was of the right
shape and size, lay on the direct road between Aleppo and
the Mediterranean, lay probably on the junction of that
road with the N-S route to the Hittite country and to Syria,
and, most important of all, because it was close to the
entrance of the Antioch valley and so commanded the road
to the sea and in all likelihood therefore owned the harbour
at the river's mouth; and, lastly, by its position on the E-W

road, close to the foot-hills, it could control the whole of
the eastern trade in the cedar-wood of the Amanus. It was
indeed self-evident that whereas Egypt got its hard-wood
from the forests of Lebanon, the timber being shipped in
coasting vessels from the Phoenician harbours of the south,
Mesopotamia, a country as treeless as Egypt, depended
largely (as ancient texts prove) on the northern forests of
Amanus, whence the timber would be hauled to the nearest
reach of the Euphrates and then floated down river to its
destination. And only by way of the Amq plain was road
haulage of the sort really feasible; this was the shortest
road to the river and the only one that was tolerably level;
if anyone wanted to control that all-important trade he
would have established himself precisely where the mound
of Atchana stands.

If, knowing nothing at all of its history, one could assume
that the Amq plain had once been a kingdom, then it was
fairly certain that Atchana had been the royal city; as such,
it was more likely than other mounds to yield historical
information. Accordingly I refused the offer kindly made
to me by my friend Claude Prost, the French Inspector of
Antiquities, to excavate the neighbouring mound of
Ta'yinat, where Syro-Hittite carvings of the eighth century
B.C. had just come to light, and asked for a concession for
Atchana and for its harbour, the little mound of Sheikh
Yusuf at the mouth of the Orontes. Of the work at the
harbour, al Mina, I shall speak later (v. p. 172); here it is
enough to say that, unfortunately, all vestiges of the early
settlement had been swept out to sea by the Orontes
changing its course and, though we did subsequently obtain evidence that it had been the port of Atchana at any
rate from the eighteenth century B.C. onwards, all that we
found on the site dated to long after 1200 B.C., a period
with which, as I have said, I had felt that we were not concerned; it is perhaps humiliating to have to confess that the
results were some of the most interesting obtained by the
expedition. Atchana, while it more than fulfilled our hopes

in most respects, did not go back to the earliest days of the Amq; it was a relatively late foundation, established at the beginning of the Bronze Age proper, not much before 3,000 B.C.; its record had therefore to be supplemented by the excavation of two little mounds in the immediate vicinity which carried the story back to the latter part of the Neolithic period.

In the seven seasons for which we were at work in the Hatay we dug therefore on four different sites, and as a result we obtained a more or less continuous history of the district from the early part of the fourth millennium before Christ to the time of Alexander the Great, the end of the fourth century B.C. It is not merely the domestic record of a petty kingdom of North Syria; because that kingdom was a border state in touch with the great empires of the Near East they too played their part in its story and the study of Alalakh is of importance for the light that it throws on the politics and the economics of the Eastern Mediterranean states. The international character which its geographical position imposed upon the site was strikingly paralleled by present-day conditions. When we started work it was in the Sanjak of Alexandretta, a North Syrian province administered by the French; in 1939 we found ourselves in the autonomous Republic of the Hatay; in subsequent years we were in Turkey. Our foremen, Hamoudi and his two sons Yahia and Alawi, were Syrians from Jerablus, the ancient Carchemish; a few of our workmen were Arabs, many more were Turks; the most numerous were the Alaouites, followers of the one pagan religion that still survives on the Mediterranean coast; there were some Kurds, a certain number of Christians of the Greek Orthodox Church, descendants of the old Byzantine population, and a sprinkling of Armenians; such a medley of races and of creeds has been typical of the Hatay since the beginning of things.

CHAPTER II

The Periods before Alalakh

*

IT was in the 1947 season that one of our workmen, a Kurd who lived in a village some three miles west of Atchana, came to me and with a broad smile said that he had something for which he expected me to pay him a really big *baksheesh*, something older than we had ever found or ever would find at Atchana, and he produced from his knotted handkerchief a collection of painted potsherds which fully justified his claim. He had been going home, and where the track cut through a low rise of ground had stooped to pick up a stone from the steep bank, and to his surprise found it was no stone but a piece of painted pottery, and then saw that there was plenty more to be got by scrabbling in the soil; his brother, who had once worked for the American expedition which excavated Tell Ta'yinat, had recognized the ware as the oldest found there, and had told him to bring it to me, so here it was, and what was I going to do about it? Naturally, I had to pay; and that is how we came to dig at Tell esh Sheikh.

The mound lay two miles west of Atchana, on the other side of the Orontes river, and was so small as to be scarcely recognizable. Once it must have been quite a considerable hill, but its lower slopes had been buried to the depth of fifteen feet by the silt deposited over the plain when the earthquake blocked the river's exit, and the ploughshare, the wind, and the rain had loosened and spread the upper soil until now its denuded top rose to no more than a

man's height above the plain; but it was an encouraging
site because, as the potsherds on the surface showed, it
had never been inhabited in historic times and therefore
would yield prehistoric remains undiluted and easily
reached.

We began by digging a trench to the SE. of the
mound, clear, as I hoped, of the village proper. The reason
for this was that we were dealing with new material and it
was best to amass as much as we could in a short time so as
to accustom ourselves to it and get a comprehensive idea
of all the varieties of pottery that the site might contain;
the houses would give us a stratified sequence, which is
essential, but on the other hand houses are sometimes so
cleanly swept that there is little left in them to show of
what the sequence should consist; nowhere would potsherds be so abundant as in the village rubbish-heap,
and since the prevailing wind blows from the NW.,
rubbish would assuredly be thrown to the SE. of the
houses. So we started by digging the rubbish-heaps, doing
our best to date the sherds by their position, and afterwards
we were able to check and amplify our conclusions by a
systematic dig in the village itself. The mound contained
twelve distinct building levels, one above another; this
meant a long period of occupation, for mud-brick houses
are reasonably long-lived, and even if one allows an average
floruit of only thirty years (which is the very minimum)
eleven rebuildings would imply for Tell esh Sheikh an
existence of three and a half centuries; and the contents
of the successive strata gave a very clear picture of the
development of the culture of the inhabitants during that
time.

The owners of the lowest and earliest houses, built on
'virgin' soil, i.e. on the original flat surface of the Amq plain,
were still, apparently, living in the Stone Age. Palaeolithic
man lived in caves or rock shelters in the hills where game
could be hunted and no trace of him is likely to be found in
the marshy lowland. But when man learnt how to domesti-

cate animals and to till the soil for food, then he must needs leave the hills for the fertile plain, and the building of houses is the natural sequel of the farmer's sedentary life. The rich well-watered Amq must have attracted settlers as soon as this change in man's habits came about, early, that is, in the Neolithic Age, and many of the mounds in the plain seem to go back to those most primitive days – it was from one of them that there came the remarkable figure of polished stone figured on Pl. 1 a, a 'Mother-Goddess' of a type found in Stone Age settlements widely scattered throughout Europe. But Tell esh Sheikh was a late foundation, dating to the very end of the Neolithic period. So far as we could judge – we excavated only a small area – it was a simple, not to say a poor, village in the ruins of which we found nothing but rough stone implements and broken pottery; the latter hand-made of plain black clay with, apart from occasional burnishing of the surface, no attempt at all at decoration. The interesting and historically important point is that this kind of pottery occurs in Neolithic strata in northern sites, in the plain of Cilicia, in Anatolia, and in the extreme north of Syria, whereas it is quite unlike the Neolithic pottery of southern Syria and Palestine; we are therefore justified in saying that the earliest occupants of the Amq plain were a people with northern affinities, probably coming from the Anatolian highlands, quite distinct in origin and in traditions from their southern neighbours. The whole course of its history shows – and indeed is explained by – the fact that Alalakh moves within the northern orbit; we can now see that the distinction goes back to the very beginning.

Accordingly the early contacts of Tell esh Sheikh were with the north and with the east to which geographically it lay open. In Level XI the same locally-made black pottery still prevails, but mixed with it are sherds of a very different ware, the painted pottery of Tell Halaf. This pottery, called after the place where it was first found, is the product of a people much more advanced than the original settlers of

Tell esh Sheikh; they were in the Chalcolithic phase of civilization in which, while stone is still used for many or indeed most of the needs of daily life, men have learned how to smelt copper and hammer it into tools or weapons; the metal is still rare and costly but its introduction has meant that all sorts of things can now be done which were impossible when only stone tools were known; it marks a great step forward in civilization. The Tell Halaf ware is hand-made but extremely fine, the best examples being of almost egg-shell thinness; its surface is usually smoothed and burnished and it is decorated with designs, in a rather lustrous red or black paint, which are often elaborate and always effective. The country which produced it was the northern strip of Mesopotamia, from Carchemish on the Euphrates (where some of it was made – the kilns have been found there) eastwards by way of Tell Halaf in the upper valley of the Sajur river almost to the Tigris; it must have come to the Amq plain in the course of trade, and it is likely enough that the eastern traders who brought it were in search of timber.

The earliest painted pottery at Tell esh Sheikh is therefore imported. To people accustomed to the plain black plates and bowls supplied by their own potters the Tell Halaf ware must have been extraordinarily attractive and the local industry was soon forced to compete with the foreigner; we find rather coarse and clumsy imitations of Tell Halaf vases which by their clay and by the quality of their paint betray themselves at first glance; but that was in the early days, and the Amq potter with surprising adaptability was, by the end of the Level XI period, manufacturing copies of Tell Halaf ware which it is difficult to distinguish from the genuine article, while the Neolithic black ware went out of production. There was indeed the likelihood that so far as its ceramics were concerned the Amq would become merely a western extension of the Tell Halaf province, but before that could happen a new influence was brought to bear on the local industry. Over the greater part of Mesopotamia –

everywhere except in the extreme north – there was being made what is now called the al 'Ubaid pottery, hand-turned vessels with, for the most part, a greenish-white surface decorated with geometrical patterns in black or brown paint; it developed rather later than the Tell Halaf ware and was not nearly so fine, but it enjoyed a wide extension and a long life.[1] This pottery begins to make its appearance in the Amq plain, and here I think that we can with confidence assert that international trade was responsible. It was not a case of foreign conquest, because the pottery comes in gradually and there is no break at all in the continuity of life at Tell esh Sheikh. All through later history Mesopotamia was to obtain its hard-wood from the Amanus forests, and though we have no written evidence to show when that trade began it was certainly flourishing as early as any written documents that we possess, and from the time when the Mesopotamian peoples were civilized enough to build palaces or temples (and the ruins of al 'Ubaid temples have been found) they must have needed timber; the mere presence of al 'Ubaid pottery at Tell esh Sheikh, on the main timber route, is the strongest possible argument for this commerce between east and west.

The importation of a rival ware to that of Tell Halaf had an interesting result. The Tell esh Sheikh potter, instead of imitating now one style, now the other, dropped copying altogether and basing himself on both schools of art pro-

1. In her book *Arrest and Movement* Mrs Frankfort observes that 'the village settlements of the al 'Ubaid period produced nothing more aesthetically remarkable than mediocre pottery painted with abstract patterns. This chalcolithic 'Ubaid culture stretches with depressing monotony from the Persian Gulf to Northern Iraq and appears to have remained stagnant for many centuries'. Actually the ware when it was first introduced into Mesopotamia was well and lavishly decorated, as is proved by specimens from the lowest levels at Eridu, south of Ur, which is an older site than al 'Ubaid; but it soon degenerated. Mrs Frankfort's condemnation of it really applies only to the later phases, but as it was in the later phases that it was imported into the Amq plain what she says is literally true for our record.

Fig. 3. *Designs on Tell esh Sheikh pottery*

ceeded to evolve a highly individual style of his own. In Level X all or practically all the painted pottery that we found is of local manufacture and, as the reproductions on Fig. 3 prove, as artistic as it is original; the motives used are always abstract, but the design as a whole is invariably adapted to and would seem to have been dictated by the

shape of the vessel to be decorated, while the calculated
balance of dark and light colour produces an effect which
in the al 'Ubaid pottery is conspicuously lacking. The craftsmen of the Amq show here an initiative, amounting to
genius, which was a good omen for the future; at the time
it would appear to have commanded commercial success,
for their wares circulated widely and are found as far afield
as Mersin in Cilicia, a fact which again proves that at this
early date the Amq, with its suggestive land and sea routes,
was already engaged in foreign trade. It is true that the high
standard reached in Level X was not uniformly maintained
and that in the upper strata much of the painted pottery is
but a slovenly and a mechanical reflection of the first fine
output of the local kilns; but that may have been largely a
question of mass production to meet an increased demand,
and does not prove that the original spirit was dead; in fact
one of the most attractive types, the first in the second row
on Fig. 3, makes its first appearance in and is characteristic of
Level II, at the close of the Tell esh Sheikh period. Nor was
the artistry of these people confined to their pottery. Though
writing was unknown yet personal seals cut in steatite or bone
were in demand for marking private property – a lump of soft
clay spread over the lid of a pot or on the knots of the rope
that tied up a basket would be stamped with the owner's
seal for security against pilferers – and examples of such
found in successive strata illustrated the development of
carving in relief. On the earliest seals we find geometrical
patterns rudely scratched on the surface of the stone; then
they are better worked, technically, and more formal in
design, and a plant or flower motive may be introduced;
then animal forms come in, some of them being very vivid
and realistic (Pl. 1 b), and one (broken) seal gave us at last
the human figure; by this time the art of working in stone
was thoroughly understood and artistic conventions were
becoming fixed, so that we find two small steatite carvings
of rams' heads, highly stylized, which evidently conform to
a recognized type; they may well be religious symbols. In

the space of some centuries the settlement of primitive farm-labourers had evolved into a sophisticated community with well-established traditions of civilization, in touch with the greater world but preserving none the less its individuality and its peculiar brand of chalcolithic culture.

Then, quite suddenly, the end came. In the surface soil of Tell esh Sheikh we found a few sherds of Bronze Age pottery and two rubbish-pits of the same date had been dug down into the top chalcolithic stratum, but such were hundreds of years later in date and only emphasized the fact that during all that time the old village site had been uninhabited. Our work there, well rewarded as it was, had yet supplied no link of any sort with our main site at Atchana; we had therefore no connected history but a record of the Chalcolithic period and then, between it and the foundation of the Bronze Age city of Alalakh, a gap in time whose length we had no means of guessing. By a stroke of great good luck Mr Sinclair Hood, who was on the staff of the Expedition, remarked just at this moment another very little mound to the east of Atchana where he picked up potsherds of a kind that had been reported from other sites in the Amq plain but had not occurred either at Atchana or at Tell esh Sheikh. A small-scale excavation on this mound, Tabara al Akrad – 'Kurds' Hillock' – filled up our historic gap and, in addition, gave us, I think, a most illuminating side-light on ancient history.

The characteristic pottery of Tabara is what is called, after its original find-spot in Palestine, Khirbet Kerak ware. It is a hand-made pottery, as a rule rather thick and heavy, occasionally red all over, more often black, but quite often the two colours are combined so that the inside of a bowl may be red and its outside black or a pot may be red below and black above; both the red and the black wares are highly burnished; where there is decoration this consists in simple geometrical motives – vandycks and so on – either in relief on the vessel's surface or produced by broad impressions with bands of shallow relief between them giving a ribbed and fluted effect; it is a very striking ware and quite unmistakable (Pl. 2). In Palestine it has been found on a number of sites. It appears fully developed and has no previous history in that country; generally it occurs immediately above a stratum the buildings in which have been destroyed by fire, and all excavators in Palestine are agreed that it is a foreign, probably an Anatolian ware, introduced by armed invaders who massacred the old inhabitants of the Palestinian villages and settled themselves in the burnt ruins; judging by the relatively small depth of deposit either the conquerors did not remain very long or, as is more likely, they mingled with the survivors of the old stock and did not for long preserve their characteristic handicrafts. In the Amq plain their pottery has been noted on nearly fifty mounds, and there excavation shows that their occupation of the area, while it began suddenly, yet lasted for a considerable time – at Tabara it is represented by four building strata. Far away to the east, in the southern Caucasus, Russian excavators have found the same pottery, but there it is in vast quantities which apparently illustrate the evolution of the ware from the simpler fabrics of the Neolithic period; the southern Caucasus would seem to have been the original home of the Khirbet Kerak people. The dispersion of their pottery over so wide an area calls for explanation, and the explanation must take into account the further (and curious) fact that while it has obvious affinities but is not identical with early wares of central Anatolia yet a single example of characteristic Khirbet Kerak pottery was found in each of the Hittite 'Royal Tombs' at Alajahüyük in Cappadocia. Those tombs date from about 2,000 B.C., and at that time the Khirbet Kerak ware was no longer in current use amongst the Hittites, so that the examples of it found in the royal tombs must be a survival perhaps due to ritual motives. But even after 2,000 B.C. the Hittites at Kultepe were still using a very curious type of clay hearth (or pot-stand for placing over the fire) which is beyond question a descendant of those used in the southern Caucasus and in the Amq plain. In my opinion there is only one interpretation of the evidence which meets it at all points; I do not imagine that it will prove at once acceptable to all the scholars who have put forward different theories as to the origin of the Hittites, but I feel fairly certain that it must be broadly speaking true.

The Khirbet Kerak people originally lived in the south Caucasus area where, starting from the Neolithic stage, they had built up a chalcolithic culture of their own of which the pottery is the outstanding feature. In the latter part of the fourth millennium before Christ events of which we know nothing at all – perhaps drought and famine, perhaps invasion by some stronger tribe – drove them from their country and forced them to seek a home elsewhere. They must have moved *en masse* with their wives and children, as has happened time and again in the great migrations of the Near East, for had it been a mere band of warriors there would have been no potters with them to carry their technique to the new lands; and they moved eastwards, probably by the easiest and most open route across northern Mesopotamia, skirting the foothills of the Anatolian mountains, not stopping, so far as we know at present (this would account for there being no Khirbet Kerak pottery in the Khabur valley through which they must, in my theory, have passed), until they came to the fertile valley of the Amq. Here was a desirable land which could be taken over by the simple expedient of putting its old inhabitants to the sword – it was the same problem as faced the Hebrews in the Land of Promise – so they took it over and lived there for many generations. Then history repeated itself. A new land-hungry people surged into the Amq from the East and once more the Khirbet Kerak folk were dislodged and driven to win fresh homes for themselves by force of arms. Two roads of escape were open to them, one leading south, one west; accordingly some of the fugitives went down through Syria and Palestine and seized villages here and

FK–2

there, slaughtering the owners and building new huts for themselves on the burnt ruins of the old; some fled through the passes of the Amanus and by slow degrees pushed northwards until, as they grew stronger and won allies, they were able to set up a kingdom and to found an empire. For in the Khirbet Kerak people we must recognize the ancestors of the Hittites. In the Old Testament Hittites are described as settled in Palestine in the days of Abraham, long before the Hittite empire came into being and extended its influence into that country. The references have therefore generally been dismissed as anachronisms introduced into the narrative by some late scribe, but that is difficult to maintain because in at least two instances the Hittites are mentioned in connexion with incidents which were almost certainly recorded in contemporary documents;[1] if, on the other hand, the Khirbet Kerak people were Hittites, survivors of them would certainly have been living in Palestine in the patriarchal age. As regards Anatolia, it has long been recognized that the Hittites were a Caucasian stock which moved thence into Asia Minor. Now they cannot have made that move directly from east to west, firstly because the successive barriers of mountain chains running north by south make a mass migration almost impossible, and secondly because they would not have been allowed to do so; even when they were established in Cappadocia and had become one of the great military powers they still could not overcome the savage mountaineers, the Gasgas, whose territories lay between them and the Caucasus; they must have made a detour to the SW. just as I have said the Khirbet Kerak people did. Moreover the scanty historical records that survive to us are sufficient to show that the Hittites made their way up into central Anatolia from the south, establishing a new capital

---

1. These are, the purchase of the cave of Machpelah, for which there must have been a contract-tablet forming the title-deed, and the marriage of Esau to 'daughters of Heth' for which again a marriage contract would have been drawn up in writing.

with each stage of their advance, in which case if they
came originally from the Caucasus they must have passed
through the Amq plain; and when in the tombs of their
early princes we find that the only pottery vessels amid all
the wealth of gold and silver are of Khirbet Kerak ware
then we can hardly fail to identify them with the people
who brought that pottery with them from the Caucasus to
the Amq and later were driven from the Amq to find new
homes elsewhere. The case is not yet proven; we have still
to find the Khirbet Kerak ware at the various stages of the
Hittite advance through Asia Minor; but the work at
Tabara al Akrad has gone far towards solving the vexed
question of Hittite origins.

It has done more than that. The mound was found to
contain seven occupation-levels of which only the upper
four are characterized by Khirbet Kerak pottery. In the
lowest stratum, Level VII, there was unearthed a substantial
building of mud brick wherein the pottery and small objects
corresponded to those from the upper levels of Tell esh
Sheikh; this gave us the continuity that we desired – Tabara
was the direct successor of Tell esh Sheikh in point of time.
In the next two levels, VI and V, there appears a new type of
pottery which both by its ware and by the forms of the
vessels is closely related to the 'Uruk' pottery of southern
Mesopotamia, evidence again of the contacts which the
Amq maintained with that country. In Mesopotamia the
'Uruk' pottery follows directly on the long-lived al 'Ubaid
ware which, as we have seen, had inspired the Chalcolithic
potters of Tell esh Sheikh, and it was in use for a long
period, though we cannot possibly say for how long. Its
occurrence at Tabara immediately above the late Tell esh
Sheikh level is in harmony with the Mesopotamian sequence.
Since it was replaced by the Khirbet Kerak ware after only
two occupation-periods its *floruit* at Tabara is very much
shorter than in Mesopotamia; either it reached the Amq
only towards the end of the time during which it was being
manufactured in the east or, as is more probable, it arrived

there reasonably early but was forcibly suppressed by the
Khirbet Kerak invaders;[1] if the latter be true then it would
mean that the invasion took place during, and fairly early
in, the 'Uruk' period which archaeologists are agreed in
placing in the latter half of the fourth millennium B.C. This
would accord with the evidence of Atchana, where Level
XIV (the third occupation-level after Tabara) is contemporary with the 'Jamdet Nasr' period which in Mesopotamia
follows on that of Uruk; although there can be no question
of exact dates when we are dealing with the illiterate phases
of pre-history we can, as soon as a relation between the
sequences in the two countries has been established, accept
for the new site the general chronology which wider experience has evolved for the other.

In the uppermost Khirbet Kerak level at Tabara there
were found a few fragments of pottery, both plain and
painted, which resembled those from the lowest level (XVII)
at Atchana; they were not made by the Khirbet Kerak
potters but were 'strangers' introduced from some other
factory, for they were different from the Khirbet Kerak
wares not only in style but in technique, since they had been
thrown on the wheel instead of being made by hand. There
were very few of them, and they were confined to the top-
most level; it would seem that such had scarcely begun to
make their way into the village when the village itself
ceased to exist. Above the ruins of those last houses there
was a barren stratum, mere agricultural soil, and then, close
to the surface, scanty remains of a settlement of the Iron
Age; it meant that Tabara had been suddenly deserted and
its site had been left uninhabited for nearly a thousand
years. The pottery fragments showed that this desertion
coincided with the incoming of the new race which built
a new town for itself a Atchana, a race that enjoyed the

1. The Level V building was over part of its area separated from
those of Level IV (Khirbet Kerak) by a stratum of burnt ashes, but
this was not uniform enough to constitute proof that the whole village
had been burnt, as in the case of Palestinian settlements.

free use of metal and turned its clay vessels on the potter's wheel; it was before this formidable invader that the Khirbet Kerak people, ignorant savages in comparison, fled to the south and west.

I have attempted to interpret the evidence afforded by two small village sites, and it would be quite wrong to pretend that my conclusions, however true they may be for those sites, apply equally to the whole countryside. Tell esh Sheikh was one of very many settlements, widely spread and not all of them necessarily confined to the Amq plain, and though Tell esh Sheikh was in the end completely deserted that does not mean that all the people who shared the Tell esh Sheikh culture disappeared. Similarly not all the Khirbet Kerak people were expelled from the Amq; Tabara was too close to the new town at Atchana to be suffered to exist for long, but other villages may have been tolerated and their inhabitants who preferred surrender to flight may have been kept on as serfs and tillers of the soil for the conquerors. The later history of Alalakh – and indeed of North Syria – is much more intelligible if we can assume that the population was a mixed one, the North Syrian element preponderating and as a rule holding the reins of power but faced always by a minority whose racial sympathies were Hittite; the assumption can fairly be made although excavation at Tell esh Sheikh and Tabara has given us only the more dramatic aspects of the story.

CHAPTER III

The Beginnings of Alalakh

Levels XVII–XIII

*

THE excavation of the two small mounds, Tell esh Sheikh and Tabara al Akrad, was, as I have said above, essential if we were going to trace the history of the Amq plain back to something like its beginning, for our main site, Atchana, was first occupied only in the Bronze Age. That fact was none too easy to establish; indeed, it involved excavation of a sort which I had never before had to attempt.

In order to obtain a record of the lower levels we chose a site in the residential quarter of the town where work had already reached a considerable depth. The top six levels had given us house sites more or less well preserved and below them we had exposed the SE. part of the royal palace of Level VII; here we marked out an area measuring about sixty-five by fifty feet for what we called the 'Stratification Pit' and dug down systematically through a well-marked succession of palaces and private buildings until we had reached Level XVI; by that time we were much below the level of the surrounding plain and the soil had been getting wetter and wetter; it was difficult to distinguish the mud brick of the walls from the mud-brick debris that enveloped them, and when we tried to go down below the Level XVI floors we found ourselves in water. Fragments of pottery embedded in the mud showed that the lowest occupational strata had not yet been reached, but it was very doubtful whether enough would be left of the flimsy house walls (which were of mud brick only, with no stone foundations) to enable us to recognize any levels at all, and the relative depth at which pottery or other objects might be found would be but dangerous evidence for dating because it would be largely accidental – a potsherd lying flat might be in its original horizon while one on edge might have sunk in the liquid mud from a much higher level. Consequently, disappointing as it was not to have fulfilled our purpose, I decided to stop the work.

But only some fifty yards away from our 'Stratification Pit' the excavation of the successive temples resulted in another great pit of equal depth; actually the pavement of the Level XVI temple was found to be flush with the floor of the Level XVI houses, and when we pulled up some of the terra-cotta tiles of the temple pavement there again was the water; we tried to go deeper, but the water poured in more quickly than we could bale it out and the sides of our trench, being of soft mud, broke away above and oozed inwards below and progress was impossible. But it was quite clear that buildings did go deeper, and since temple walls were much more solidly constructed than those of a private house there was a better chance of distinguishing them even in such difficult conditions, and in any case a temple site was too important to be lightly abandoned; the work had to be interrupted, but only until we should be better equipped to deal with its problems.

The buildings had of course originally stood on dry ground; that they were now submerged was due to the blocking of the Orontes' channel and the raising of the level of the Amq plain to which I have referred before, but the level of the water-table is not constant; we were digging in the spring, when it is at its highest, and the summer drought would lower it appreciably. We therefore changed our digging-season and came out in the autumn. We brought petrol-driven pumps, and on the temple pavement we built, with steel girders and corrugated iron sheets, a large caisson inside which eight or ten men could work; as they dug and as the pumps emptied out the water the caisson sank of its own weight into the mud and there was no possibility of the men being hurt by the caving-in of the sides. The water-table had been lowered three feet since the spring, which was an advantage, but it would have availed us little had we been digging in the open; as it was, working inside the caisson, we could without any great difficulty go down fifteen feet and more below the Level XVI temple pavement. I say 'without any great difficulty', and that is true enough from the engineering point of view – indeed the whole scene at the pit's bottom with its pumps and pipes, derricks and pulleys, ladders and strutted platforms, looked much more like an engineer's workshop than an archaeological excavation – but archaeologically speaking it was not altogether satisfactory. The ordinary rules of scientific digging could not apply when semi-liquid mud had to be scooped up in buckets; it was quite impossible to observe anything *in situ* – at the best of times the men were ankle-deep and sometimes, with an inrush of water from below, they were waist-deep in a sort of pea soup in which nothing could be seen; it was only by examining the harder lumps in the buckets that we could tell whether we were dealing with mud brick or with loose soil. None the less the results obtained were well worth the labour involved, and since we dug down in this way in two distinct spots we could check our evidence and make sure of our conclusions.

In the first place, virgin soil was found to lie just about fourteen feet below the tiled pavement of Level XVI. A solid block of mud brickwork, the top of which was visible in Level XVI, could be traced down with certainty for ten and a half feet and probably (though conditions at that depth were such that we could not be sure) went further down to rest on virgin soil. We could not make out whether this block was homogeneous throughout or had been built in stages representing different periods, nor could we distinguish any floors or surfaces in the soil in front of the block, though behind it there did seem to be a more or less regular succession of strata of clean soil and of mixed rubbish which should mean either gradual accretion or perhaps repeated levellings and re-floorings; on the face of it a rise in level of more than ten feet should imply not one building-period but several, but one cannot assert that this was necessarily the case. All the potsherds, etc., collected in the course of the work, were therefore lumped together and described as belonging to Level XVII; they may really belong to two or more successive levels, but they are all older than Level XVI and – and this was the most important of our results – they take us back to the beginnings of Atchana when newcomers to the Amq plain set up their first buildings upon virgin soil.

All the pottery characteristic of Tell esh Sheikh and of Tabara al Akrad had been hand-moulded; all the pottery in Level XVII at Atchana is thrown on the potter's wheel. In the top level at Tabara a few imported sherds of Atchana fabric occur, enough to prove continuity, but there is no mistaking the fact that the settlement at Atchana meant the introduction of a culture absolutely different from anything that had preceded it in the area. Taken as a whole the Level XVII pottery is different again from that of Level XVI, but it is a difference of degree rather than of kind; we do not find there the finely-painted wares with bird and animal motives which are characteristic of the upper levels, but we do find the beginnings of that style, rather rough and simple attempts at painted decoration, so that what followed implies not a revolution but a natural development from the primitive art of the first settlers. Who those settlers were we cannot as yet say. They had achieved a relatively high degree of culture, knowing all about the potter's wheel and freely using and smelting metal – we found in Level XVI their stone moulds for casting copper adzes – and building very solid structures of mud brick, but they do not seem to be connected with the other stocks about whom we know anything; they are definitely not Mesopotamian or South Syrian, nor do they appear to have anything in common with Anatolia, those being countries whose archaeology is tolerably familiar to us; it is quite possible that such a culture may have developed not very far away from the Amq, in the Aleppo plateau for instance, where there have been no excavations to tell us about the early periods, and that its arrival in the Amq was the natural expansion of the higher civilization at the expense of the lower. It can hardly have been a peaceful expansion, for the people of the Tabara time would not have relinquished their lands without a struggle; it is noteworthy that their pottery fails completely from now on – not a single sherd of it has been found at Atchana – and also that the new-comers did not settle down in the old villages but, as if to accentuate the breach between past and present, founded their city on a virgin site. That some of the Tabara people did not take part in the exodus which scattered those 'Proto-Hittites' into Palestine and Anatolia is proved by the specimens of 'imported' Atchana pottery mixed in the top-most level of the mound with the Khirbet Kerak ware, but there could be no question as to who was master of the Amq. A new era had begun. So far as we can tell, the old population had lived in villages which might indeed be of some considerable size but were, all the same, merely the villages of an agricultural and simple folk. The men of the Bronze Age laid the foundations of a city, which in time came to be called Alalakh (unless they so called it from the start) and amongst the first buildings which they set up was the temple of the city's god. The city was to endure for something like two thousand years, and during those mil-lennia the temple was to be rebuilt not once but fifteen times on different patterns and to different gods, but no reformer ventured to shift the cult centre from the site sanctified by the builders of the city's earliest shrine.

Of the temple itself all that we found, perhaps all that still exists, is a cube of solid brickwork some sixteen feet square and thirteen feet high – though the height may have been much less at first and added to by later builders as the ground level round it rose. Against its NW. face there was a thick deposit of ashes, animal bones, and potsherds which must be the remains of sacrifices. Whether the cube was an altar or not we cannot tell, but it was peculiarly sacred, for when in due course the Level XVI temple came to be built

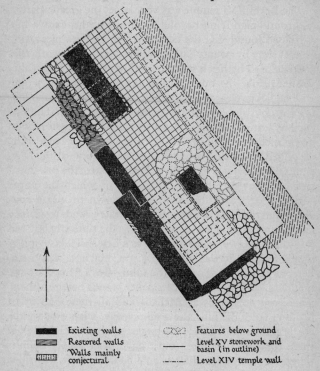

	Existing walls		Features below ground
	Restored walls		Level XV stonework and basin (in outline)
	Walls mainly conjectural		Level XIV temple wall

Fig. 4. *Plan of the Temple of Level XVI*

high above the ruins of the original shrine this cube was carefully preserved; part of it rose above the new building's floor, a smaller rectangle rather more than six by three and a half feet (it may have been a new work resting on the old, but we could distinguish no change in the brickwork) and this was neatly topped with a pointed roof of timber; in front of it there was a square opening in the pavement, a pit of which the lower part was filled with great stones but above them ashes and animal bones, proving that the old sacrifices were continued on the same spot.

The Level XVI temple was very large, the greater part of its ground-plan lying beyond the limits of our excavation. What we found was the central court, an area measuring at least sixty by twenty-one feet, paved with terra-cotta tiles and enclosed by brick walls smoothly plastered and white-washed; since the outer face of the walls also was white-washed it was clear that there had been chambers surrounding the court, but we know nothing about them. The two curious features of the court were the brick structure with its pointed roof and pit for sacrifice which I have already described, this being towards the SE. end, and, at the NW. end, something yet more mysterious. Before the pavement was laid they dug here a square pit, of which the upper part at least was brick-lined, going down to virgin soil; we found this, of course, full of water, and it seemed natural to describe it as a well, but at the time when it was dug there was no water and it was a dry shaft. As soon as it was finished it was filled up again, but not with earth; here, as in the sacrifice-pit, the filling was of huge stones, boulders, with a packing of smaller stones between them. There are no stones at Atchana and all these had to be brought from the hills a few miles away, a laborious and a costly matter seeing that the largest of them weighed over three tons, so that there must have been a very definite religious motive for their use. When the shaft was filled and levelled the floor tiles were laid over it and then on the tiles there was built a free-standing mass of brickwork eight feet high, really a stretch of wall eighteen feet long and five wide with a low doorway, flat-lintelled, through the centre of it, but the doorway, though carefully con-structed, was blocked with brickwork and plastered over so as to be completely hidden. One end of the 'wall' rested on and coincided exactly with the stone-filled shaft. The brick mass – we called it the 'mastaba' on the analogy of Egyptian tomb-superstructures having false doors, but the parallel does not really hold good – with its blocked doorway and its obvious association with an underground shaft laboriously filled up as soon as it was dug presents us with as pretty a problem as an archaeologist could desire; it was something essential to the worship that went on in the temple, of that we can be sure, but beyond that we cannot go as yet. What the ruins do tell us is that the early Bronze Age people kept to the religion of their forefathers, seeing that they based their altar for sacrifice (if we may so interpret the roofed brick structure) immediately on that which had served the Level XVII temple, and that the religion was peculiarly their own, owing nothing of its form either to Mesopotamia or to Egypt. In a Level XVI house we found a slate palette (for eye-paint) closely resembling those found in Egypt in the middle Pre-Dynastic period and this, if we can trust an isolated object, should imply a contact – though not necessarily a direct contact – with the Nile Valley. But that does not mean that the Amq was at that date under Egyptian influence; of the two countries the Amq was indeed the more advanced. Already in Level XVI the experiments made by the first settlers in the painting of pottery had been perfected; the potters were now producing such admirable vases as the jugs shown on Pl. 3 and had set a fashion which was to prevail for a thousand years. From now on, until the eighteenth century B.C., the same shapes and the same patterns were to characterize the finer pottery of Alalakh, and so rigidly was the tradition followed that unless we know the level at which a painted vessel was found we may be unable to date it on stylistic grounds within a millennium; for such obstinate conservatism I can quote no parallel.[1]

1. The willow-pattern plate has had an astonishingly long vogue in England, over a hundred and fifty years, and shows no signs of losing its popularity; but will it endure for a thousand?

The wealth and initiative of Level XVI were followed by a phase of decadence; there was no evidence of any disaster, no violent overthrow or burning of houses or temple, but rather a stagnation; old buildings were patched and mended when neglect and decay had brought them to a state that really called for reconstruction; such scanty remains as we can attribute to the period have a very sordid air. Phases like this may occur in the life of any city, but there is always a reason for them. Here it is perhaps possible to find a parallel and an explanation in what was happening in Mesopotamia. There the Uruk period had been one of great advance and prosperity; the Jamdet Nasr period which followed it was, judging at least by its art (for of its political history nothing is known), dull and uninspired. The Jamdet Nasr people were certainly newcomers who by fair means or foul imposed themselves on the country and could not, at first at any rate, assimilate the superior culture of the older inhabitants, though in time they developed sufficiently to prepare the way for the fine achievements of the Sumerians of the Early Dynastic Period which came after. Now Level XVI at Atchana is contemporary with the latter part of the Uruk period, Level XV with the beginning of Jamdet Nasr, and I am inclined to correlate Alalakh's changing fortunes with the demand for timber due to the great building programme of the later Uruk rulers and to the trade slump that may well have resulted from the Jamdet Nasr invasion.

But as conditions improved in Mesopotamia so they did in the Amq. Our Level XIV falls within the Jamdet Nasr period, as is conclusively proved by our finding in its house ruins a number of examples of a particular type of clay bowl which has been recorded on many sites and invariably in the Jamdet Nasr level. Its occurrence here is of course direct evidence for contact with Mesopotamia, so that the relation which I have assumed hitherto now becomes a historical fact; there is no question of conquest, the relation must have been one of trade only, and as the

Jamdet Nasr people prospered and progressed the trade is likely to have assumed large and, for Alalakh, profitable proportions. Consequently in Level XIV we find the city temple completely rebuilt, and the remains in the Stratifi-

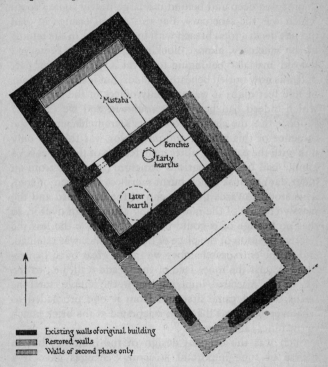

Fig. 5. *Plan of the Temple of Level XIV*

cation Pit showed that in the residential area also new houses were constructed which were much more solid and better planned than those of the previous period, while the great amount of finely-painted pottery witnessed to the wealth of the time. Like the houses, the new temple did not follow the constructional lines of its predecessor. On a

raised terrace formed by filling in and levelling the old
ruins there rose a simple building consisting of an open
forecourt enclosed by a parapet wall and, facing on it, the
temple proper, an entrance-chamber a good deal wider
than it was deep and behind it a large nearly square room
which was the sanctuary. But this radical change in plan
did not mean a total breach with tradition, for in the middle
of the sanctuary, almost blocking it, there was preserved
the old 'mastaba' belonging to Level XVI; the lower part
of it was now buried beneath the floor, but it still stood four
or five feet high; it was the only object in the sanctuary,
which indeed had been built round it, and we can only
suppose that the chamber owed its sacred character to the
presence of this relic of antiquity. Nor was this the only
link with the past. The other main feature of the Level XVI
temple had been the curious structure (inherited from an
older day) against which burnt sacrifices had been offered.
This stood towards the SE. end of the courtyard and the
massive façade of the new building actually ran over it, so
that no vestige of it could be seen, but none the less the
relative position of the place of burnt sacrifice was retained,
and in the entrance-chamber we find a great oven or fireplace against the inner face of the façade wall, i.e., to the
SE. of the 'mastaba', implying that in the temple ritual the
burnt offering came first and from it one proceeded to
whatever act it was that men celebrated at the brick bench
in the inner sanctuary.

Such was the original design of the building, but in
course of time important structural changes gave it a
somewhat different character. Against the inner face of the
back (NW.) wall of the sanctuary there was added a skin of
new brickwork so thick that it blocked completely the
passage-way between that wall and the 'mastaba'; so, at
the same time, the whole of the space between the 'mastaba'
and the NE. wall was filled in with brickwork, turning it
into a great platform which took up a full half of the area
of the room. In the entrance-chamber similar brick 'skins'

were added to the two end walls, giving them a thickness of over seventeen feet; the SW. skin was plain, but that at the NE. had a deep central niche, while a broad brick bench was built against the NW. wall. The obvious reason for thickening the walls was that their height might be increased, and one can imagine the temple as taking the form of a lofty tower, but the remodelling of the interior suggests something more than that, for in the sanctuary the substitution of a solid platform at one end of the room for a free-standing central pedestal should imply a change of ritual, and the niche in the end wall of the outer room, with the bench alongside, makes it look as if this had been turned into a cult chamber; at the same time the floor of both rooms was raised and in the open forecourt a new brick pavement was laid at a higher level. Here we had a curious side-light on temple practices. The original courtyard had been on two levels; against the temple façade it was flush with the threshold of the entrance-door, but at a distance of ten feet from it it was stepped down eighteen inches and the floor of this lower area was of clay only as against the mud-brick pavement of the upper part. We found this lower area filled (under the brick pavement of the later phase) with a deposit of rubbish – ashes, animal bones, and fragments of clay pots, the throw-out of sacrifices; it is of course possible that when the alterations took place this rubbish was brought here and put down as a bedding for the new pavement, but it is more likely that it is a gradual accretion and that it had been the regular habit to throw away what was left after sacrifice into the temple court. To us such disregard of mere litter may be shocking, but it is quite in keeping with the insouciance of the Near East – and after all the litter was in this case consecrated matter. A point of interest was that one of the pottery fragments came from a standard lamp (as we now know it to have been) of what has been called the 'champagne-glass' type which is very common in tombs of the Early Bronze Age at Carchemish – there over sixty examples

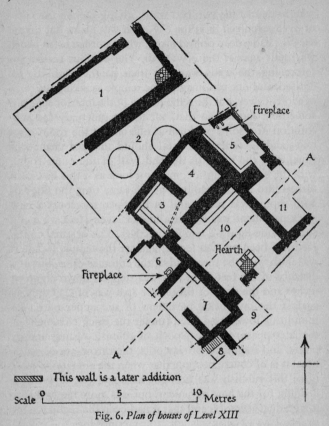

Fig. 6. *Plan of houses of Level XIII*

have been found in a single tomb[1]; its occurrence on the
Atchana temple site establishes a link between Alalakh and

1. This was inexplicable as long as the purpose of the 'champagne-
glass' was unknown, but when specimens found in the Level VII
temple at Atchana proved to be lamps, the meaning became clear.
In rock-cut tombs of early Christian times at Carchemish we had found
as many as a hundred lamps of Roman form, and it is obvious that
lighted lamps were deposited in the grave by mourners as symbols of
resurrection.

Carchemish which is important because the cultures of the two cities have generally very little in common.

The temple I have described corresponds to two distinct building-periods in the residential area illustrated by our Stratification Pit. There Level XIV seems to coincide with the temple's foundation, but it is followed by a Level XIII in which new houses are constructed at a higher level and on a different plan and, in particular, at the NW. end of the excavated area, there came to light part of a building of a much more solid and pretentious type (Fig. 6), a single room of which was almost as large as a normal house. One very valuable piece of dating evidence was forthcoming. I have said that Level XIV must be correlated with the Jamdet Nasr period in Mesopotamia; a room in the Level XIII house produced a cylinder seal engraved with the 'banquet' scene which in subject and in technique is quite typical of the first half of the Early Dynastic period which followed Jamdet Nasr. For the house site then, Levels XIV and XIII are distinct. I think that we can safely associate the rebuilding in the town with the remodelling which, while it left the old temple standing, did so materially change its character, and can therefore attribute the new version to Level XIII; it would be not at all surprising if the massive walls of the temple outlived two generations of private houses; they might well have lasted much longer had not political reasons ordained otherwise.

CHAPTER IV

The Foundations of the Kingdom

Levels XII–VIII

*

WITH Level XII a new chapter in the history of Alalakh begins.

When we dug down to this stratum in our Stratification Pit we were greatly puzzled at finding a circular mass of mud brickwork about six feet six inches in diameter; the top was broken, but the sides were smoothly mud-plastered. Then a second was found, close by, and a third and a fourth, all more or less in one line; and finally we discovered that we had to deal with a row of huge columns built of mud brick and standing in front of a very heavy wall behind which was a high brick-paved platform dominating the smaller houses which lay at a discreet distance from the colonnade in the southern half of our excavation (Pl. 4). The discovery was a surprising one because no such brick columns were known to have existed in any place or in any period in Syria; here was something without any local precedent and, so far as we know, without any successors in Syrian architecture. The only parallels we could cite lay far afield. In Mesopotamia, at Warka, the Biblical Erech, there was a palace façade adorned with huge columns built of mud brick and overlaid with mosaic; those were standing in the Jamdet Nasr period; at Kish, further south, a palace of the Early Dynastic period had a hall down the centre of which was a row of similar but plain brick columns; apart from these there is nothing.[1] But in the Level XII temple there were found two engraved cylinder seals of Early Dynastic type, Mesopotamian or copied from Mesopotamian origi-

Fig. 7. *Plan of the Palace of Level XII*

nals, and these are enough to prove firstly that our Level XII falls within the Early Dynastic period, and secondly that in that period the two countries were in contact; the Alalakh

1. There is a slender (attached) mud-brick column at Ur, but it is of a wholly different character and a thousand years later in date (it is the work of Kudur-Mabug, King of Larsa) and therefore does not concern us here.

columns then were derived from Mesopotamian prototypes.

A building too important, one would think, to have been
the house of an ordinary private citizen, had, in Level XIII,
occupied the site of the colonnade, and from now onwards
until Level VII this was to be the site of the royal palace;
there can therefore be no doubt then as to the nature of the
building to which the Level XII colonnade belonged. For
a long time the wealth of the city had been increasing as a
result of its eastern trade, and when a nationalist rising in
Mesopotamia put an end to the foreign Jamdet Nasr régime
and there emerged from the struggle those rich, ambitious,
and artistic city States which made the Early Dynastic
period the finest, perhaps, in the history of the Euphrates
valley, that trade became more profitable than ever, and
the ruler of Alalakh richer in proportion. Whether the
succession was peaceful or, as is intrinsically more likely, a
palace revolution led to the change from Level XIII to
Level XII, the new king decided that he must be becomingly
housed in a manner different from his predecessors and,
naturally enough, borrowed for his palace the architectural
ideas of his business clients in the more civilized East; the
exotic colonnade whose discovery so astonished us is indeed a monument to international commerce.

It was wellnigh inevitable that a new dynasty should set
up a new temple; either the ruler had his own particular
patron god who must be given due eminence, or the god of
an ally or overlord must be propitiated or, if nothing else,
piety to the traditional gods was a form of insurance for
his continuing in power. The Level XII lord of Alalakh
made no exception to the rule. There is no reason to suppose
that the massive walls of the existing temple were in such
bad repair that they could not have remained in use for
many years, but the temple building as such was now out of
fashion; the only thing to do was to destroy it and build
afresh. On the other hand there may have been certain
religious qualms about the gratuitous destruction of a

time-hallowed shrine – at least it is only in this way that I can interpret what we actually found. The Level XIV temple, as re-used in Level XIII, had not been destroyed by fire; the whitewashed faces of the inner walls and of the façade showed no trace whatsoever of burning. But the outer face of the SW. wall[1] had been burnt; the entire face of the brickwork was smoke-blackened and sticking to it were numerous fragments of light brushwood, all completely carbonized. The curious point was that fuel of that sort, fired in the open, would make a fine blaze but would not set up any great heat and certainly could do no harm to such massive walls – as a matter of fact the red discoloration due to fire did not penetrate for more than half an inch into the brickwork – and that after the fire the place had been carefully cleaned – there was no burnt wood at all lying on the ground. Long before we understood the nature of the building we had come to the conclusion that this was a ritual fire intended to give the effect of destruction by fire, whereas really all that had happened was that the building was temporarily blotted out by a curtain of flame; and I believe that this is the true explanation. The brushwood was heaped against the sanctuary walls and set alight and the old building was symbolically 'destroyed', after which work could go ahead without scruple. The ashes were swept away, the walls were cut down to a height of some ten feet above the old floor level, and then inside the rooms and round the outer walls bricks were laid, the usual mud bricks in mud mortar, until a solid platform was formed, incorporating all that was left of the former temple, and on the top of it the foundations of the new temple were laid. It was of the same size as the last and like it had a sanctuary building of two rooms, but its whole effect was entirely different. The front of the platform was masked by

1. This was the only wall, apart from the SE. façade, of which the outer face was exposed by our excavations, so that I can speak only of that; but it is likely enough that the same is true of the back and other side walls.

a steeply-sloping *glacis* revetted with white plaster, a northern invention which recurs several times at Alalakh and was
to be carried south by migrant tribes until it appears in
Egypt at the Hyksos stronghold of Tell el Yahudiyeh, capital
of the Semitic invaders who for a spell lorded it over the
conquered valley of the Nile. One entered by steps near the
south corner and passed along a passage into a little room

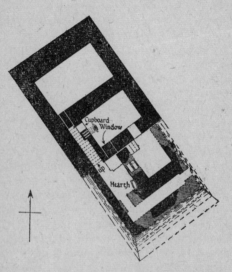

Fig. 8. *Plan of the Temple of Level XII*

or forecourt where there was a fireplace for burnt sacrifice
and two doorways; one of these, on the right, led into
another small room or court on to which opened the front
room of the sanctuary block; the other was the doorway of
a passage filled with a flight of wooden stairs going up to
the shrine proper. For the building was not on one level. As
first built, all the floors were flush, the back chamber having
a carefully smoothed clay floor which was presumably used
for some service of dedication; but immediately afterwards

brickwork was laid over that floor to a height of fourteen
and a half feet so that the chamber could be entered only by
the stairs – with the front room it had no connexion at all,
but probably a door led out from it onto the roof of the
front room so that part of the shrine's ritual could be conducted in the open air and in the public view. From the
outside then the building had a stepped effect, the courtyard[1] forming the lowest element, the outer chamber rising
up above it, and the sanctuary proper, like a church tower,
dominating the whole. At Selemiyeh in central Syria there
has been found a clay model (Fig. 9) of a temple which
supports and amplifies this reconstruction based on the
existing remains of our Level XII building; it gives the
sanctuary block only, without the forecourt buildings, but

Fig. 9. *Clay Model of a Temple from Selemiyeh*

illustrates very well the lofty back chamber whence a doorway leads onto the roof of the front room; the model-
maker has not troubled to reproduce the staircase, but he

1. I have described the divisions of that area as rooms *or* courts; it is
quite possible that they were roofed, but since they were construction-
ally independent of the temple block and since at one time the interior
walls were dismantled, leaving the whole area as one necessarily open
space, it is reasonable to assume that a distinction was carefully made
between this subsidiary part and the main sanctuary block.

does show – what the ruins do not – a certain amount of decoration of the outer walls and also the windows in both rooms, whereas at Atchana only the sill of one window in the front chamber was preserved. The temple type is neither Mesopotamian[1] nor Egyptian; since it occurs at Selemiyeh as well as at Atchana it can fairly be called North Syrian, but bearing in mind the relation between North Syria and the Hittites, we may perhaps see in it the prototype of the 'Hittite' *Hilani*, a high building with windows, which later in history so took the fancy of the Assyrian kings that they were prone to set up imitations of it in their own lands.

Level XII lasted for a very long time. So far as the private houses are concerned it includes three distinct building-periods, and we should have described them as of three different levels had it not been for the fact that the palace with its colonnade is contemporary with them all; this gave a unity which we could scarcely disregard. But the palace itself, judging by the tiny fraction of it which was all that we could clear, was twice remodelled in that period and the great columns had to be repaired at least twice. One of them must have collapsed fairly early, for its foundations were unstable, resting half on the Level XIII wall and half on mere accumulated rubbish, while a palace drain emptying just at this point still further weakened the subsoil, so that the shaft began to lean outwards at an alarming angle and had to be propped with a rather clumsy skin of new brick-work added to its circumference. This may have been at a time when the monarchy was under a shadow, for the houses of the second phase overstep the old limits of private property and are built right up against the colonnade, showing no respect for the royal palace and completely masking its main architectural feature. But in the last phase

1. Some early clay models from Asshur might be connected with our building, but they are generally taken to represent houses, not temples; of all the Mesopotamian temples that have been excavated not one presents any analogy with Level XII at Atchana.

the king comes into his own again; the encroaching houses are swept away, leaving in front of the palace a wide open space as at first, interrupted only by a new one-room building which may have been a guard-room, and the colonnade was rebuilt; the row of columns was prolonged (originally there were only four and now we find a fifth, with its foundations at a higher level) and the old shafts were cut down almost to the (new) ground level and fresh shafts built on the stumps;[1] the ups and downs of fortune are aptly illustrated by the vicissitudes through which the palace passed. In the same way the Level XII temple was twice remodelled. There is no need to assume that changes there synchronized exactly with the phases of building in the residential quarter; what is important is that they confirm our view that the level as a whole represents a very considerable lapse of time. Levels XIII and XII together must correspond to virtually the whole period of the Early Dynasties in Mesopotamia, i.e., from very early in the third millennium down to the middle of the twenty-fourth century B.C.; it is absolutely consistent with such dating that we find in the palace of Level XI a seal-impression on clay which on grounds of style could belong either to the close of the Early Dynastic period or to the time of Sargon of Akkad whose reign, according to the shorter chronology now generally accepted, began about 2320 B.C. Granted in the first place that a seal might be in use for a long time and, in the second, that a sealed document might be long preserved, we should hardly err if we conclude that the year 2300 B.C. came within the Level XI period.

In Level XI both temple and palace were rebuilt. Of the former we can say no more than that, for all that bears

---

1. The builders were evidently worried about the leaning column and distrusted it as a base; so instead of merely trimming the top flat they cut into it a deep cup-like hollow and laid the foundations of their new shaft in that; it was a curious expedient and seems to show that the local builders were dealing with a form of architecture which they did not really understand.

witness to it is a mass of mud brickwork filling the rooms of Level XII to make a platform for the new temple; but of its superstructure not a vestige survives. The palace, of which we laid bare only about six rooms, had been much enlarged and extended over the area where had been private houses;

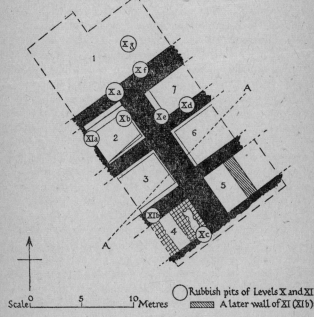

Fig. 10. *Plan of Palace of Level XI*

it seemed to have taken the form of a triple range of chambers surrounding a central court; some of the rooms had pavements of burnt tiles, the walls were extremely thick, and voussoir bricks scattered over the building seemed to show that the rooms were roofed with barrel vaults, a constructional method which had been used in Mesopotamia since Early Dynastic days but has never before been recorded in Syria. Here we have evidence of a change of dynasty and the introduction of foreign practices which can, I think, be explained by the prosperity of the previous age. The king of Alalakh owed his riches, in good part at least, to the hard-wood trade and it may well be that, encouraged by its expansion towards the end of the Early Dynastic period, he had opened his mouth too widely and was charging exaggerated prices or imposing exorbitant dues on goods in transport. That policy might succeed with the ordinary rulers of the city states along the far-off Euphrates, but at this time a new power had arisen in northern Mesopotamia, and Sargon of Akkad was not a man to submit tamely to extortion and, as we know from his own records, he was keenly alive to the importance of foreign trade; impatient of middlemen's charges he marched westwards with his army and forcibly annexed the Amq and Amanus, getting the sources of supply into his own hands. It is to Sargon's conquest that I would attribute the destruction of the Level XII buildings, and it is even possible that the new palace, with its rooms vaulted in Mesopotamian style, was set up to house the governor or vassal king installed by him.

It was not easy for Akkad to maintain its suzerainty over a place so distant as Alalakh and once at least there was a rebellion which had to be crushed by Sargon's grandson, Naram-Sin, who boasts of his triumphal march to 'Amanus, the mountain of cedar, and to the Upper Sea'; all this may have taken place in the period of Level XI without leaving any distinguishable mark upon the city's buildings. But twenty-four years after Naram-Sin's death the dynasty of Akkad came to an end, overthrown by the barbarous Guti, and then, if not before, Alalakh could reassert its independence. Moreover it could resume its profitable business. The very looseness of the Guti rule and their failure to organize a centralized government ('Who was king? who was not king?') allowed a good measure of liberty to the local rulers, so that Gudea of Lagash can boast of the huge baulks of cedar-wood that he imported from the Amanus for his temple to Ningirsu. In Level X we find the ruins of an entirely new palace, again constructed with vaulted chambers in the Mesopotamian tradition, and again the temple was rebuilt, though nothing more than its platform remains to us. The same is true of Level IX, which should synchronize with the Third Dynasty of Ur, and there, in the palace ruins, we found a seal bearing an inscription in cuneiform of what is called the Kültepe type, i.e., similar to the many texts discovered at Kültepe in Cappadocia where there was a colony of Mesopotamian merchants trading with the local ruler. It is likely enough that a certain number of Mesopotamian business firms had their resident agents at Alalakh; it would be rash to argue on the strength of a single seal that they formed a regular colony as at Kültepe, but since our work was confined to the palace area no trace of such a foreign settlement could be expected and the finding of even one isolated seal is at least symptomatic; but there is no mention of Alalakh in the Kültepe texts.

In the Level VIII period a new and very large temple was built of which only the fire-reddened and crumbling walls are left; on the palace site there was only a remodelling of the former building. Nothing was found in the stratum that could throw light upon the political history of the time, but we can none the less recover its main outlines with tolerable certainty. In various Syrian towns, and as far north as Ugarit which is only some forty miles from Atchana, there have been found monuments of the Egyptian Pharaohs of the XIIth Dynasty. Those energetic kings embarked upon a policy of foreign conquest which carried their arms far afield; the first blows were struck by Sesostris I and his grandson Sesostris II was, by about 1900 B.C., in possession of virtually the whole of Syria;[1] his empire bordered on, if

1. At Ugarit there are scarabs of Sesostris I, but the earliest large-scale stone monuments (and only those are unquestionable evidence) are of Sesostris II; to him therefore the capture of the city is more safely attributed.

it did not actually include, the city State of Alalakh. No contemporary monuments of the Pharaohs have been found at Atchana, but the negative argument is not final and wider excavation might well reveal such; but in the following period we have evidence of 'Egyptianizing' traditions which are most illuminating – a royal portrait is modelled on an Egyptian prototype (Pl. 6 b), a member of the royal family is represented on his seal carrying Egyptian emblems and worshipping an Egyptian god. These survivals (for such they were) can only mean that a little while before, and for some considerable period, Alalakh had been directly or indirectly under Egyptian influence; either its ruler had been a vassal of the Pharaoh or, if he maintained a precarious independence, it was at the cost of aping the fashions and flattering the gods of his powerful neighbour. In either case, Level VIII marks the preponderance of Egypt, and that endured until, about 1790 B.C., a weaker Pharaoh saw the Empire slip from his grasp and the Syrian kinglets were left free to play their own game.

Up to this point our history of Atchana has been of a very sketchy sort. The excavation of these early levels involved digging down to a depth of more than fifty feet, the cost of the work increasing at every foot, so that the area covered was necessarily small. The great 'Stratification Pit' was, as its name implies, undertaken merely to give us an idea of the number and character of the underlying levels; the other and deeper shaft was due, in the first place, to a misunderstanding, for we had cleared the Level VII temple and, suspecting that it might be a mortuary chapel, I gave the order to go down on the chance of finding a royal tomb and since we encountered nothing but solid and apparently homogeneous brickwork went ever deeper; it was only after a long time that I realized that we were in fact passing through the superimposed remains of many temples belonging to as many periods where there was nothing in the nature of the expected tomb but, instead, a vast amount of unexpected historical information. But the two shafts, which

by good fortune supplemented each other admirably, giving
us the parallel sequences of temples and residential sites,
were yet nothing more than *sondages*, trial pits serving a
limited purpose; they supplied precisely that which one
hopes to get from a trial pit, successive building-strata each
with its content of pottery and small objects, material which
enables one to mark cultural changes in a historical order
whose phases can be defined by the buildings. We were
more than usually successful in that we were able in so
many cases to correlate the successive periods with historical
facts already known, thanks to the presence of imported
objects or borrowed fashions which linked Alalakh to the
outer world, and so could establish, what a *sondage* seldom
justifies, an approximate chronology instead of a mere
sequence divorced from time.

The contacts we have observed were, until about 1900
B.C., exclusively with the east;[1] this is but natural, seeing
the geographical position of Atchana and in view of the
fact that from the beginning of the Bronze Age the population was a mixture of northern and eastern strains, the
latter preponderating, and that little was to be learnt from
the still barbarous north whereas the east was the birthplace
of one of the oldest civilizations and therefore bound to
exert an influence across its frontiers. What is remarkable
is the continuity of pottery types and especially of the
painted wares. These, as we have seen, originate as a local
product and are already fully developed in Level XVI, and
during the next thousand years they persevere without a
trace of foreign influence. Although, in Level XIV, there
occurs a particular form of ritual vessel of Jamdet Nasr
origin, we have found not a single example of the characteristic painted pottery of Jamdet Nasr nor any modification
of the local patterns that could possibly be referred to it. In
Mesopotamia, throughout the Early Dynastic and Sargonid
periods and under the Third Dynasty of Ur, the pottery is

1. The one possible exception is the palette found in Level
XVI.

very unimaginative and painted decoration is virtually lacking; the Alalakh potter therefore could draw no inspiration from the east and, faced by no competition, could safely go on producing replicas of the really superior wares made by his forebears.[1]

1. Taking the forms of vessels only, irrespective of decoration, twelve types are common to Levels XVI and VIII, twenty-four occur before Level XII and not after it, nine occur between Levels XI and VIII but not before XI. But it must be remembered that the evidence is very partial, and had we dug over a larger area the proportion of types common to all levels might have been considerably greater.

CHAPTER V

The King of Yamkhad
Level VII

*

WITH Level VII our history assumes a wholly different form, and that for two reasons; in the first place, we were digging at no very great depth and so could extend our work over a large area and recover entire buildings, and in the second place we now for the first time found tablets written in cuneiform; our history therefore is based on much fuller archaeological evidence and we have the inestimable advantage of supplementing that evidence with the literary record.

The buildings of the period which we excavated are the royal palace, the city temple, and the city gate, so that we have a good idea of its civil, religious, and military architecture; in the palace and the temple numerous tablets were found; those, though of course only the chance survivors of a vastly greater number, are fairly representative of the official archives. All the tablets fall within the reigns of three kings, Hammurabi, Yarim-Lim, and Niqme-epukh, the total of which need not be much more than fifty years; the majority of them belong to the time of Yarim-Lim, a contemporary of Hammurabi the great king of Babylon who reigned from 1792 to 1750 B.C.;[1] Yarim-Lim seems to have died some time before Hammurabi of Babylon's

1. According to Professor Sidney Smith. Professor Albright has put forward a slightly different chronology whereby Hammurabi's reign is from 1728 to 1686 B.C. This cannot be reconciled with the evidence from Atchana and I have therefore adopted the earlier date and follow Sidney Smith's chronology for everything down to the end of Level IV.

thirtieth year and we may provisionally date his reign as between *circa* 1780 and 1765 B.C.

Undoubtedly it was the collapse of the empire of the XIIth Dynasty of Egypt that made possible the aggrandizement of its old vassals, and when the field was thus left free for them there must have been a great reshuffling of thrones and frontiers. By some 'exchange' the city of Alalakh passed into the hands of one Abban, a shadowy character who appears to have been the founder of a new dynasty; he was the father of Hammurabi king of Yamkhad and the grandfather of Yarim-Lim. Yamkhad was a considerable kingdom, lying to the east of the Amq, the capital of which was Aleppo (the king was called 'King of Yamkhad' or 'King of Aleppo' indifferently) and the extension of its territories to the shores of the Mediterranean vastly increased its importance. By a deed of gift Abban settled this new domain not on his son but on Yarim-Lim. It was a regular custom for Middle Eastern rulers to entrust the government of vassal cities to their brothers or sons, thus minimizing the chances of conspiracy against themselves, and such was presumably Abban's intention – Hammurabi as King of Aleppo would have his court in the traditional capital while Yarim-Lim as his regent would govern the Amq from Alalakh. On his father's death Yarim-Lim succeeded to the whole kingdom. An interesting testimony to his importance is given by a tablet from Ma'er (Mari) containing an intelligence report sent to Zimri-Lim, the king of that city; the agent states that 'there are ten or fifteen kings who follow Hammurabi of Babylon and ten or fifteen who follow Rim-Sin of Larsa' (these being the two great rulers of Mesopotamia at that time) 'but twenty kings follow Yarim-Lim of Yamkhad'. The suzerain of twenty vassal kings could play a leading part in the power-politics of the day and Yarim-Lim seems to have been an adroit, not to say unscrupulous, player, siding now with Babylon and now with Larsa as occasion served, but keeping his own lordship intact against all rivals.

Of the tablets that we found relatively few give the name of Hammurabi, the vast majority are of Yarim-Lim, but many of those record the activities of one Ammitaku who as civil governor was responsible for the city's finances. The Hammurabi documents must go back to the time when Yarim-Lim was regent for his father, the others must represent the archives of his own reign, and although authority was undoubtedly delegated at times to Ammitaku the fact that the archives were kept at Alalakh would seem to imply the king's presence there. The character of the Level VII buildings excavated by us points to the same conclusion. All are nearly if not quite contemporary and can safely be attributed to Yarim-Lim; he may of course have started to build a palace for himself while he was yet only his father's viceroy, but the later additions to the palace (it was constructed in successive phases), the temple and, above all, the massive fortifications should be the work of a reigning and a resident monarch. Faced with the dangerous ambitions and the uncertain alliances of the Mesopotamian Powers Yarim-Lim may well have thought that Aleppo, lying towards his eastern frontier, was unduly exposed to surprise attack and therefore, while retaining it as his principal city, have transferred the seat of government to the capital of his old province, making his home there and bringing its defences up to date.

At the extreme NW. end of the mound of Atchana we sank a trial trench (this was in the last days of the excavations when there was no time left for digging on a large scale) which proved that this part of the ancient town was throughout all the later levels occupied by a great fortress, the citadel in which the military garrison was housed. We went down just deeply enough to get evidence that this was true of Level VII also, and since with each rebuilding the general character of the defences remained constant we can safely say (though only a tiny section of his work was laid bare) that Yarim-Lim's fort was a mud-brick structure standing on a platform raised well above the

level of the rest of the town so as to command the approaches
from the north and west and, on those sides, formed the
main inner line of defence; from the foot of the fortress
wall there stretched a gently-sloping berm about fifty feet
wide on whose edge was an outer wall, probably of no
great height, and then a steep glacis, built of brick and
faced with a clay revetment, sloped at an angle of rather
more than forty-five degrees, twenty-six feet high. The
sloped glacis which we first met in the Level XIV temple,
where it was on quite a small scale, has here been elaborated
into a military work of a most effective character; it was as
unclimbable as a vertical wall and had the advantage that
an enemy coming up against its foot was still in the direct
line of fire instead of getting a certain amount of protection
such as a wall affords, whose defenders can shoot only by
leaning over the wall's top and exposing themselves to the
archery of the attacking force. An enemy who succeeded in
carrying the outer wall would still find himself on a sloped
berm which gave an ideal field of fire to the garrison of the
fortress. It was a method of fortification which seems to
have originated in North Syria, for a measured description
of the defences of a North Syrian town which is given in a
text of Naram-Sin of Babylon[1] agrees remarkably well with
the actual ruins discovered at Atchana, so that the type
goes back long before the time of Yarim-Lim; but it is
difficult to imagine one better suited to the conditions of
warfare then in vogue.

The NW. gate of the city – probably the main gate
seeing that it gave on the great road between Aleppo and
the Antioch pass – immediately adjoined and was commanded by the fortress. From the plain a fairly steep
approach led up to a massive gate-tower set between the
outer wall of the fort and the city wall, on the same line as
the latter, so that its upper chambers might serve as a
passage-way between the two sections of the defences; the
road passing through the tower was blocked by triple

1. C. J Gadd in *Ur Texts*, Vol. I, *Royal Inscriptions*, p. 81.

gates (Pl. 5 (a)). Here again there is nothing original; the
gateway is of the type approved by military experience,
almost a replica of the main city gate of Carchemish, with

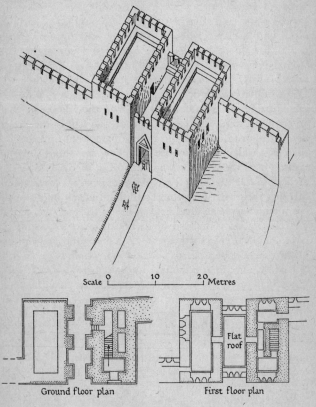

Fig. 11. *The Town Gate of Level VII*

which it is virtually contemporary, and in its general lines
closely resembling a number of other gates known to us in
the Middle East of both earlier and later periods.

The gateway ruins which we unearthed were, naturally, those of the lower part of the building only, but they were sufficiently well preserved to make its general character quite certain (Fig. 11). The tower as a whole was built of mud brick set in a frame of heavy beams – the half-timber construction which is typical of Hittite work; but the façade both on the inside and on the outside and the doorway reveals, as well as the massive piers of the three gates, had a lower course of finely-dressed white limestone blocks standing as much as four feet high. The stones of the pier ends were not upright but sloped slightly inwards, suggesting a form of gateway like that of the Hittite capital, Bogazköy in Cappadocia; in that case the pointed arch above the sloped jambs was corbelled, which is the natural method where the building-material is stone, but here a similar effect could have been easily obtained with half-timber construction, though it can safely be assumed that there would have been a flat lintel below the false arch. One side of the tower was solid, being in fact the corner of the huge rampart of the citadel, but the other, the NE. half, had in its inner wall a wide doorway with stone jambs and steps leading into a guard-chamber; at the back of the room a flight of stairs, the lower treads solidly built in brick and the upper of timber, led to the room above the gate and so to the top of the city wall; below the stairs there was a little chamber with a door set between the outer and the middle piers of the gateway, obviously a sentry-box for the guard actually on duty. This sentry-box is a curious weakness in an otherwise admirable design, for an enemy had only to force the first of the three great doors of the gate-tower to be able to enter the sentry-box and by setting fire to its wooden roof destroy the stairs and probably the entire building. Something of the sort seems to have happened, for the tower had in fact been destroyed by fire – the guard-chamber had been gutted and the mud-brick walls of the staircase were burned to a deep red colour and the clay floor of the gate passage was covered with a thick layer of burnt wood which must have been the floor of the room above; the gate-tower had not proved impregnable.

We were not able to excavate any of the city wall, but there can be little doubt as to its character. The royal palace stood at an angle of the town and two of its outer walls were in fact the town walls; they were of mud brick and were eight feet thick, rising from the edge of a steep-sided earth rampart about thirty feet high – the height is given by the height of the palace floors above the plain outside; that the rampart was of earth, not of brick as in the case of the citadel, is argued from the fact that all later ramparts were of earth, sometimes revetted with clay, and that there was no berm but the wall rose directly from the edge of the slope seems to be proved by the fact that all the outer face of the NE. wall of the palace has disappeared, fallen away down the slope. Whatever had been the case before, in the eighteenth century B.C. Alalakh could rank as a first-class fortress, and in it, on what had long been the traditional site of the royal palace, Yarim-Lim built a new palace for himself. It was a time (not the only one in Middle East history) when local princes vied with each other in the splendour of their houses; thus the ruler of Ugarit writes to Yarim-Lim asking him to arrange for him to see the palace of the King of Ma'er because he had heard so much of its magnificence, and the King of Yamkhad, like Nero, was determined to be housed as a gentleman should be. To-day the SE. end of the building, the domestic part, is too ruined for its plan to be recovered, but even so the area covered by the palace measures 320 by 50, feet so that for its size alone it was imposing (Fig. 12). The only entrance, a doorway in the middle of the long SW. side, led into a large open court extending right across the building up to the town wall; slabs of polished basalt formed a dado round the walls; in the centre was a raised square hearth; in the wall on your right there were two doors and on your left, in the far corner, a single door giving access to the state apartments. The palace was built in two parts separated

by the courtyard and the character of the rooms makes it
quite clear that these were respectively the official and the
private quarters. The middle of the official block was taken
up by a Chamber of Audience, a long room divided into

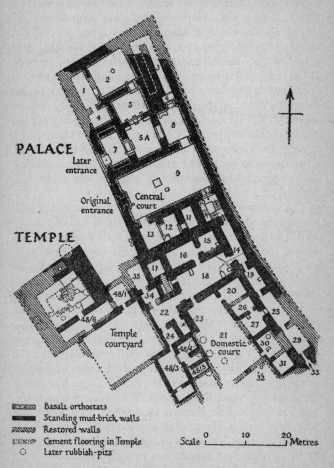

Fig. 12. *The Palace of Level VII*

two by piers projecting from the side walls and a row of four wooden columns resting on a concrete threshold – the black circles left on the concrete by the burning of the shafts were clear to see. The outer, or public, part of the audience-chamber was flanked by waiting-rooms, one of which, having a door opening from the great courtyard, served also as entrance-chamber. The inner part of the audience-chamber, reserved presumably for the king and his officers, had behind it a large withdrawing-room (perhaps at the same time a secretariat) and opening off that a small room which may have been an archive (though we found no tablets in it) and then a still smaller room which, though we could not excavate it entirely – it lay directly beneath the corner of the later palace of Niqmepa – can on the analogy of other buildings safely be identified as a lavatory. In the north corner of the block there was a great staircase leading to the upper rooms; the building was certainly of two and perhaps of three storeys.

The visitor entering the great courtyard would see on his right-hand side two doors, one at either end of the SE. wall. The first of them was the door of three communicating rooms lying at the same level as the court; they were magazines, not living-rooms, and were lighted, if at all, by small windows set very high up, for the walls were found standing to a height of eight and a half feet and showed no sign of any window opening – that store-room windows should be inaccessible was an obvious safeguard. Their floors, of smoothly plastered concrete, were deep in ashes and littered with clay tablets, the business archives of the palace, and with elephants' tusks. This throws an interesting sidelight on the economics of the period. Ivory was one of the most important 'luxury articles' of ancient commerce, and for the Middle Eastern lands there were only two sources of supply. Egypt of course could get its ivory from the south, either in the way of regular trade down the Nile or by Government expeditions passing through the Red Sea to Punt, somewhere on the Ethiopian coast. For Syria there was the Syrian elephant, now extinct but in the second millennium B.C. not uncommon; but that source was not generally available. The Syrians never attempted to domesticate the elephant, and in the whole country there were very few places where the wild animal could possibly subsist; the only area of any size where there was water and a jungle-like growth of scrub to give food and shelter was on the right bank of the Euphrates by the great bend of the river south-eastwards from Aleppo; we know for a fact that there were elephants there, and it is probable that they were corralled there in a sort of 'game preserve' in the interests of the ivory trade. Now this was in the land of Niya, and Niya was part of the domain of the King of Yamkhad; Yarim-Lim therefore enjoyed a monopoly of the northern ivory, in addition to controlling the northern traffic in cedarwood, so that we can well understand the magnificence of his palace and appreciate his reason for providing in it magazines for the storage of the precious tusks.

The residential block of the palace was built on a terrace about four feet higher than the central court. The doorway to it – the second doorway on the right as you entered the court – opened therefore on a staircase with stairs built round a brick newel; immediately inside the door there was a little lobby with, on the right, a cupboard under the stairs and on the left the first flight of steps at the top of which another door led to a long passage skirting the outer wall of the palace; the ground-floor rooms reached by this passage were for the most part of a domestic nature, kitchen, servants' quarters, and workshops, while the stairs continuing round the newel-post took one up to the living-rooms of the royal family. The block was probably three storeys high, and of the upper rooms nothing, of course, remains *in situ*, but from the debris fallen through into the magazines we can recover some idea of the principal room of the *piano nobile*. This was a saloon just over forty-five feet long (it overlay all three magazines) divided like the audience-chamber of the official block into two unequal parts by shallow piers or buttresses with wooden columns between them; at its south-west end was a large window of three lights separated by stone columns and framed in square-cut stone. The saloon, like most or all of the better rooms of the palace, had been adorned with frescoes. These have generally disappeared, leaving only the finger-impressions in the wall plaster which were for keying-in the coloured *intonaco* or surface plaster; in the audience-chamber of the official block we recovered traces sufficient to show that it had been painted with an architectural design exactly like some in the royal palace of Minos in Crete; but in the case of the saloon big fragments of the wall had slipped down, after the destruction of the floor, into the magazines below, and to some of them the painted plaster still adhered – mere fragments, but precious for the information which they yielded. The decoration was in true fresco, the wall being plastered in sections and the paint applied while the plaster was still wet – a technique which we find in Crete but never on Egyptian walls where the decoration was always done in *tempera* on dry plaster; in the main part of the room the design was on a white ground with broad bands of blue and yellow and bulls' heads (or perhaps complete figures of bulls) in black; in the SW. part, between the dividing columns and the window, there was a ground of Pompeian red with naturalistic designs of which the only recognizable fragment showed long grasses waving in the wind, quite realistically rendered in yellowish white (Pl. 6 a).

It is here, in our Level VII, that for the first time we can trace connexions with Crete, but now they are unmistakable. The methods of construction employed in Yarim-Lim's palace are the same as those of Knossos – the polished stone slabs lining the base of the walls, the half-timber construction (though in the stony island of Crete rubble naturally takes the place of mud brick), the free use of cement, the wooden columns on plain circular stone bases, even details of planning such as the lay-out of the audience-chamber; and the frescoes are identical in colouring, tech-

nique, and style. In Crete all this appears suddenly in the
palace of Minos and contemporary buildings, there being
no sign of local development, and after the Minoan age it
all disappears; but Yarim-Lim's palace is in the old tradition,
and its features are reproduced in later buildings right down
to the seventh century B.C.; moreover Yarim-Lim's palace
antedates by more than a century the Cretan examples in
the same style. There can be no doubt but that Crete owes
the best of its architecture, and its frescoes, to the Asiatic
mainland. And we can say more than this. The exchange of
goods by international trade is one thing, and a most important thing, but it has its limits; one cannot export a
palace on board ship, nor is the 'art and mystery' of fresco-
working a form of merchandise. These professional techniques require direct contacts, and we are bound to believe
that trained experts, members of the Architects' and Painters'
Guilds, were invited to travel overseas from Asia (possibly
from Alalakh itself, seeing that it had its Mediterranean
harbour) to build and decorate the palaces of the Cretan
rulers. In precisely the same way, at a later date, Cretan
artists were summoned to Egypt to paint in durable fresco
the palace floors of the XVIIIth Dynasty Pharaohs – which
is why we find Mycenaean pottery in the poorer houses of
Tell el Amarna. One of the main objects that we had in
view when we started the excavations at Atchana was to
throw light on the origin and development of Cretan art,
and it was extremely satisfactory to secure such definite
evidence of its indebtedness to Asia.

I have said that the ground-floor rooms of the residential
block were for the most part service-chambers; thus, those
numbered 15 and 18 on the plan had their built-in stone
washing-basins and drains running underneath the floors
to carry the dirty water away through the town wall;
further to the SE. where the buildings were only one storey
high (as was shown by the thinness of the walls) there were
work-rooms for the palace dependents, No. 30 being a
stone-mason's shop and 29 a pottery-store; but not all were

so easy to understand. One room (17 on the plan) confronted us with an unexplained mystery. While the palace was being built a square shaft was sunk in the ground here and in it a chamber was built with a solid concrete floor seven and a half feet below that of the adjoining palace rooms and with walls of three courses of heavy basalt blocks set in cement; in the SE. wall there was a doorway with basalt jambs and lintel and the door itself was a single slab of basalt turning on boss hinges and secured by a peg bolt inserted in a hole in the stone threshold; this door was approached from the ground surface by a narrow staircase with steps of timber, cobbles, and clay neatly covered with white plaster, the side walls being of rough limestone plastered with cement (Pl. 5 b). We found the stone door ajar but blocked by large boulders piled against it inside the stone-walled room; in one corner of that room there was a pile of wood ash in which were three alabaster and three terra-cotta vases; against the SW. wall there was a wooden box containing four human skeletons so arranged that a skull came in each corner of the box. As we found it, the sunken room was filled with clean earth; the staircase was roofed with timber and over it a concrete floor was laid flush with the floors of the adjoining rooms, the doorway at the top of the staircase was bricked up and a new door cut through the NE. wall of the room under which the stairs now lay and a doorway above-ground was built above the buried doorway of basalt; presumably a new floor was laid over the earth filling of the shaft, but if so it had all been broken up later. Thus two very ordinary-looking small rooms took the place of the underground chamber and its approach.

It is quite certain that the making of the shaft was contemporary with the building of the palace, because the rubble foundations of the palace walls actually rested on the stone walls of the shaft, and, on the other hand, the bricking-up of the doorway at the stairs' head must mean that the SE. wall above-ground was standing when the shaft was in use. But the use of the shaft escapes us. When we found the buried staircase and the basalt door we felt sure that they were leading us to a royal tomb – but there was no tomb; the ignominiously boxed skeletons and the three stone vases had nothing of royalty about them, nor, since the blocking of the door had been done from the inside, had there been any roof such as a tomb-chamber would necessarily possess. I can only suppose that this was a foundation-sacrifice, some sort of ritual that consecrated the new building ('he set up its gates in his first-born') but if that be so then the religion of the time had some most unexpected tenets.

For any disappointment that we may have felt at the non-appearance of a royal tomb Yarim-Lim's temple made full amends. He built it on the traditional site, immediately above the ruins of the temple of Level VIII the lower part of whose walls were turned to account, for they served to contain the masses of concrete which made the foundations of the new structure. The ground-plan was simple enough – a big forecourt surrounded by service chambers and, at the back of it, a single-room sanctuary, almost square, with raised benches along its sides and a stepped altar built of basalt blocks set against the bench facing the entrance. But the massive character of the mud-brick walls – they were thirteen feet thick – meant that the building was very lofty, and a staircase contrived in the thickness of the front wall and, in the thickness of the back wall, a vertical drain-stack built of burnt brick and clearly intended to serve some ritual of libations carried out in an upper chamber, showed that the temple was at least two storeys high, and it may well have been more; in any case it would seem to have been in the form of a great tower dominating the city. Like the palace, the temple had been burnt and, before burning, very systematically plundered. The benches had long wooden chests concealed under their concrete tops, and these had been broken open and emptied; the floor was littered with tablets from the temple archives, fragments of ivory inlay, and broken statuary. A curious object, found broken

into more than a hundred widely-scattered pieces, was a
drum-shaped terra-cotta brazier or vase-stand decorated
with applied terra-cotta figures, goddesses, and a human (?)
warrior represented as falling, perhaps an illustration of
some legend. There were wigs and parts of beards delicately
carved in soap-stone which had belonged to composite
statues whose faces had probably been of ivory and their
bodies perhaps of gilded wood; and there were two human
heads carved in diorite, which must have come from statues
arranged along the temple benches, of quite extraordinary
interest. One of them, badly damaged, was in the Egyptian
style (Pl. 6 b) – not an Egyptian work but made by a local
artist who attempted, not too skilfully, to achieve an Egyptian effect; the sculpture must belong to the time, just before
Yarim-Lim rose to independence, when the influence of the
XIIth Dynasty Pharaohs was still strong in Alalakh and a
member of the royal house would feel obliged to have his
portrait done according to the artistic standards of his
suzerain. But the second head – one likes to think that it is
the likeness of Yarim-Lim himself – has nothing Egyptian
about it (Pl. 7); it is the product of an entirely different
school (and therefore of entirely different political conditions) and is a masterpiece of original art. On technical
grounds one would say that the sculpture is descended
from the Sumerian art of a much earlier day; the nearest
approach to it in date and style is a magnificent bronze
head, perhaps a portrait of Sargon king of Akkad, found
at Nineveh, but that too is older than our head by some
centuries; it would seem that there must have existed,
perhaps in northern Mesopotamia, a school of art of which
we have no knowledge, ultimately derived from that of
Sumer but developing on its own lines and attaining a
standard of merit seldom equalled in the Middle East. As
it is, this head is an isolated phenomenon; but from whatever artistic centre it may have sprung it remains an astonishing piece of portraiture and a remarkable work of art.

A city such as Alalakh, the residence of a king whose

dominions were fairly widespread and his wealth largely
based on international trade, was bound to be open to outside influences of many sorts, but the foreign style of an
object found there does not necessarily imply a foreign
origin. The stone vases found in the mysterious shaft in the
palace might pass as Egyptian, but it is just as likely that
they were locally made and the stone-cutter chose Egyptian
models simply because those were what his clients were
used to. Raw materials were imported as well as finished
goods. Thus against the outer wall of a big building of
Yarim-Lim's time (we could not excavate it, for it lay
directly below the later palace of Niqmepa) we found the
workshop of a man who specialized in the manufacture of
obsidian vases. Obsidian, or volcanic glass, came from
eastern Anatolia; it was imported in the form of smoothly-
ground rectangular blocks measuring about twelve by
eight by eight inches. The workman shaped his vase by
chipping in the old flint-knapper's technique; he hollowed
it out with a solid round-ended drill, making the holes close
together and then breaking away the ridges left upstanding
between them; then the whole surface had to be ground
smooth, which gave an opaque matt effect, and finally this
was polished and the vessel took on its finished appearance
of black or bottle-green translucent glass; with that brittle
and intractable material the whole process must have been
as delicate as it was difficult, and one can well imagine that
the trade was in the hands of a few experts whose work
fetched high prices on the market.

The more we excavated the buildings of Level VII the
more were we struck by the pottery found in them. First
and foremost, the traditional painted wares which had
characterized every level from XVI to VIII now failed
completely; we did not find a single painted pot of that sort.
It is of course quite true that in times of great prosperity
the pottery of a country tends to suffer eclipse – that rich
man prefers to furnish his table with vessels of bronze,
silver, or gold rather than with the old earthenware crocks,

and therefore what had long been the luxury ware of
Alalakh might go out of fashion when Yarim-Lim was
king. But that explanation does not serve here. In the
palace and temple, and in a few private graves of the poorer
sort, we found masses of clay vessels, all plain but of many
different shapes – just over forty types were recorded – and
of them only eleven had occurred in older levels and all the
rest are introduced with the Yarim-Lim régime; there was
a very obvious break in the ceramic tradition. Moreover,
ten of those new types did not outlive Level VII; and when
we come to Levels VI and V we find that the old painted
ware has been to some extent at least revived and no less
than twenty old shapes which had been disused in Level
VII now return to favour. The break in the tradition is
therefore a temporary one, coinciding with the Yarim-Lim
dynasty.

The kings of Yamkhad were primarily kings of Aleppo;
they had absorbed Alalakh and they made it the royal residence, but they were foreigners none the less, and as such
they brought in new fashions and new arts. Probably some
of the innovations were resented; it may be that the old
painted pottery which had been characteristic of Alalakh
for many centuries could be looked upon as a symbol of
the nationalism which opposed change, and was therefore
deliberately discouraged; but it was probably only one of
many things that were swept away by the new order. The
dynasty of Yarim-Lim, for all its wealth and prosperity, incurred the hatred of the citizens to a degree that cannot have
been due to any change in household crockery but must
have had far more valid grounds. Late in the period certain
alterations were made in the palace which are symptomatic
of the growing unpopularity of the royal family and their
distrust of their subjects. The entrance-door of the central
court, from which access was had alike to the official block
and to the residential quarters, was elaborately bricked up;
a new entrance was made by cutting a doorway through
the outer wall of the SW. waiting-room in the official block

and its other walls were strengthened and it was turned into a guard-chamber through which everybody had to pass to go to the Chamber of Audience; and it was only by going through that and then through the second waiting-room (where again it was easy to have a guard) that a visitor could enter the central court and so make his way to the private apartments of the palace.

When we unearthed the building we found that it had been burnt – burnt so thoroughly that even in the core of the thick walls the mud-bricks were bright red and crumbling; the wall plaster, a mixture of mud and lime, had been vitrified and the basalt wall-slabs were not only cracked but in some cases actually melted; it had also been systematically plundered. In the new guard-chamber we found the skeletons of five armed men, and two more were found in other rooms. My first impression was that seven bodies were too few. If the palace had been stormed by some enemy from outside, which could only have been after a successful assault on the city walls, the palace would have been the final rallying-point for the defenders and would have been held to the bitter end: it ought to have been heaped with corpses. The actual conditions seemed rather to favour a surprise attack – the normal palace guard had been suddenly cut down and after that there had been no resistance and the whole building had been at the mercy of the assailants; this indicated an *émeute* by the people of Alalakh themselves. Subsequently we discovered that all the State buildings of the city had been similarly burnt – the temple, the citadel, the town gate, and the big building underlying Niqmepa's palace, and my original argument lost a good deal of its point; but it may still be true. If the military works were garrisoned by 'foreign' troops from Aleppo and the eastern provinces of the kingdom, an attack on them would necessarily have followed on the capture of the royal palace, and king Niqme-epuch is not likely to have relied on locally-recruited soldiery. On the other hand the theory of the town's destruction at some time between 1750 and 1730 B.C. by an enemy from outside presents certain difficulties, for Aleppo, the chief city of the kingdom of which Alalakh formed part, continued to enjoy its 'great kingship' long after 1700 B.C. It is true that it was a time of change and of those movements of peoples which every now and then interrupted the history of the Middle East – about now the Kassites invaded Babylonia and occupied part of its territories, and by 1730 Semitic nomads invaded the Nile valley and as the Hyksos, the 'Shepherd Kings', usurped the throne of Pharaoh, but we cannot definitely attribute the fall of Niqme-epuch to any such great event. On the whole, a local rebellion seems most plausible, and although the people of Alalakh may have been encouraged by happenings in the outer world to try to recover their independence, and may even have obtained some help from outside, I think that they were responsible for the violent end of the dynasty of Yarim-Lim.

This view gains probability in the light of subsequent events. Apart from the return to favour of the old types of pottery, in which we may see a 'nationalist revival', certain very curious things occurred. Yarim-Lim had built his palace on the site where royal palaces had stood ever since there were kings of Alalakh, and it was the most desirable site in the city. But after Niqme-epuch's death nobody built there. For 150 years the great mounds of debris and the gaunt stumps of fire-reddened walls were left severely alone, a devastated area in the midst of a crowded city, and the only use to which the ruins were put was the digging of rubbish-pits and the dumping of refuse; as if there were a curse on the king's house it was 'left unto him desolate' and became 'a dung-heap'; and when a new palace was needed for a later king an entirely new site was chosen for it. Nor was this all. Yarim-Lim's temple also stood upon the traditional site, sanctified by a succession of shrines going back to the city's first foundation, each built directly above its predecessor. But from 1730 B.C. onwards there was a change. Yarim-Lim's temple had in some way or other outraged religious sentiment; it was impossible indeed to forsake the ancient site, but it was equally impossible to found a new house of god on the abomination of desolation which he had set up. So henceforward the sanctuary of 'the goddess who is Mistress of Alalakh' stood over what had been the forecourt of the old temples while the area behind it, defiled by Yarim-Lim's shrine, remained at first altogether unused and when, some generations later, prejudice had weakened, was used only as the site for service chambers. In this studied break with everything that stood for the kingdom of Yamkhad we have the best explanation of the fires that consumed the palace and the citadel of king Niqme-epuch.

CHAPTER VI

The Dark Ages

Levels VI and V

*

YEAR after year as we dug down in one spot or another through the buildings of Level IV until we reached those of Level VII I was puzzled by the character of the intervening strata. We knew that Level VII ended not later than 1730 B.C. and we knew that Level IV began not earlier than 1500 B.C., so that rather more than two centuries came between them; but though we found two layers of buildings – which justified us in speaking of Levels V and VI – they did not seem substantial enough to account for the passage of 200 years. It was the more disappointing because the period in question was undoubtedly very important, a period, as Professor Sidney Smith has said, of remarkable development in the Near East, of which only the outlines can be vaguely surmised, and we had hoped that Atchana might go far towards filling up this gap in our knowledge. Ideally, of course, we ought to have hit upon the political archives of the city, but in fact not a single inscribed tablet was found and our history had to be pieced together out of such purely archaeological material as was forthcoming. Fortunately, in our last season, work on the Citadel site cleared up our main difficulty; it was little more than a trial trench that we dug on the edge of the town mound, NW. of the gateway, but it served to correct the wrong impression that excavation on other sites had given us. What we found there was that after the burning of the Level VII citadel there had been, in the Level VI period, a complete rebuilding of the defences, but this new work had itself been replaced by a fresh reconstruction in the course of the same period, and similarly, in the course of the Level V period, there had been two thoroughgoing reconstructions of the citadel. In each case we find the same general scheme of a strongly-walled castle set on the top of an artificial rampart with a wide gently-sloping berm running out from the foot of the wall and ending in a steep glacis on the lip of which there was probably (though the evidence for this had gone) a low breastwork. Such buildings are necessarily of very solid construction, not likely to fall quickly into decay, and though we must always allow for the possibility of any one of the series having been dismantled by a victorious enemy soon after its erection none the less we must agree that for the total period represented by four re-buildings 200 years would be a very moderate estimate. The evidence of the citadel buildings is confirmed by the pottery from that and other areas. In both levels we find imported wares which, occurring on other excavated sites in Syria, Palestine, or Cyprus, have been independently dated; in Level VI we find a Cypriote type dated to before 1650 B.C., a Palestinian type dated 1650–1550 B.C. and another dated 1600–1500 B.C. and, while the two latter continue in Level V, towards the end of the Level V period there appear the first examples of the painted 'Nuzu' ware produced in the east in the fifteenth century B.C. Thus the whole interval between Level VII and Level IV is accounted for, and if the buildings other than the Citadel appear scarcely adequate for the length of time involved, that appearance must not be given undue weight (as I was myself inclined to give it); after all, a mud-brick house if well built and reasonably well looked-after will quite easily last for 100 years. There is too another possibility that must be taken into consideration. If I am right in arguing that the public buildings of Level VII were destroyed as the result of a successful civil revolt, then there is no need to assume the destruction of private houses; the greater part of the town would not have suffered at all and people would have continued to live in their old homes until those decayed or grew out of date and had to be replaced in the normal course; that happened after the destruction of Niqmepa's palace and may well have happened in the case of Level VII also. We cannot however affirm that this is true. The only private houses of Level VII which we excavated were those overlying the ruins of the servants' quarters of Yarim-Lim's palace; there was very little of them left, not enough for the plans of them to be intelligible, but it was certain that they had been built only comparatively late in the Level VI period. That fact however has no real significance. When Yarim-Lim's palace was overthrown the ruins of the two- or three-storeyed residential block made a great mound which was continued to the SE. by the solid mass of the town wall; consequently the servants' quarters, where walls had been thin and of only one storey, formed a low-lying patch enclosed by higher ground from which any rainwater drained down so that in winter the place became a stagnant pool – we found layer after layer of dried mud bearing witness to this. Quite apart therefore from any embargo on the palace site this area was not fit for occupation and was used as a refuse-dump, becoming in time honeycombed with rubbish-pits; this gradually raised the level and finally, but only after a considerable lapse of time, people began to build there. But no argument based on conditions here can apply to the town in general. We might have got very different results if we had been able to dig more widely in the residential parts of the Level VI town, but that we could not do; the buildings lie deep down in the soil and extensive work to that depth would have meant an expenditure of time and money better devoted to the investigation of more important sites, so that here we had to content ourselves with probabilities.

Our trial trench on the Citadel site showed that there too there had been an interval between the destruction of the

Level VII building and the construction of the first building of Level VI; the burnt ruins of the former had been exposed to the weather long enough for wind to level the loose debris of brick-dust and ashes and for rain to form pools at the foot of the stumps of standing walls. This might have happened in a single winter, but may imply the passing of several years – it was impossible to say which. The uncertainty prevents us from using the facts as an argument. If the destruction had been due to an enemy it is understandable that some time should elapse before the citizens were allowed to refortify their town; if it had been due to the citizens themselves one would expect them to put the defences in order again with the least possible delay – though perhaps other and more important things had to be done first; either theory would fit the evidence according to the interpretation that we choose to put upon it.

We do indeed know extremely little about the Level VI buildings. I have spoken of the Citadel and the houses, and there was little to be said; we did not find a palace because we did not dig in the spot where the palace would have been if there were one; there was a temple, but it had been completely destroyed, only a fragment of one wall remaining.

It is to the pottery that we must look for information about Level VI, and the pottery can tell us a good deal. On the one hand we have what I have called the 'nationalist revival' of the traditional painted ware which had been suppressed under the late régime, and some examples of this are perfect replicas of the old both in form and in decoration, but as time goes on there appear modifications of the long-established types – instead of the isolated and static figures of birds or animals these become active and are combined in running scenes surrounding the whole pot without the interruption of the triglyph-like partitions which were once the rule; and at the same time the painter, using a bigger brush for his colours, obtains a much broader and impressionistic effect; vases so treated could never be mistaken for the product of early levels. The change may well be due to the influence of foreign models, for in this period pottery was imported more freely than ever before. For the first time we get a polychrome decoration in red and black paint on a buff surface, and the design includes not only birds but the 'Union Jack' motive which is specially characteristic of contemporary Palestine; some examples

Fig. 13. *Designs of Pottery of Level VI*

might be actual imports but most are local copies. Definitely imported were hand-made bowls of what has hitherto been called Cypriote Bronze Age ware, bowls derived from leather originals having handles copied from the wish-bones of chickens; in one type the clay is covered with a white slip on which the seams of the leatherwork are painted in black with subsidiary decoration in red – these are the 'White Slip milk-bowls' of Cypriote archaeology – and the other is of 'Base-Ring Ware', a thin hard biscuit-like pottery of a uniform brown-grey colour (Pl. 9). The two types were first found in Cyprus and in the Late Bronze Age of that island are so predominant that they were naturally supposed to be indigenous, the typical product of the native potter; and when examples were found abroad (as they often have been found on Palestinian, Syrian, and Anatolian sites) they were taken to be proof of trade connexions with Cyprus and, since the chronology of Cyprus was fixed without too wide a margin of error, they were used without hesitation to date the strata in which they occurred. But at Atchana we have a chronology not less well established than that of Cyprus and for our examples of the White Slip and Base-Ring pottery the Cyprus dating simply does not fit. Two wish-bone handles turned up in Level VII, and in Level VI both wares become relatively common, increasing in popularity in Levels V and IV; so far as Levels V and IV are concerned there is no difficulty, but the earliest examples date to 150 years before the time when White Slip and Base-Ring pottery appears in Cyprus. We are driven therefore to revise our views. The pottery is not Cypriote by origin. It is certainly not native to Alalakh either, because the Alalakh potter had for centuries been using the potter's wheel, whereas here we have a primitive hand-made fabric and one which in form and decoration is wholly alien to all Alalakh traditions. Judging from the clay and the pigment the bowls would seem to have come from somewhere in northern or eastern Anatolia, but that is a point which only excavation can determine; what is obvious is that they were introduced to Alalakh by way of trade and just because they were strange and barbaric attracted attention (they *are* rather attractive) and became fashionable – one might compare the vogue of Negro sculpture in modern London, or of Navajo blankets in New York – so much so that in time no house could afford to be without them. It was only after the market for such goods was well established in North Syria that someone – probably a Cypriote ship's captain – carried a consignment overseas to Cyprus, where they had the same success. The discoveries at Atchana do not in any way upset the dating of the wares in the island but do mean that outside the island that dating does not apply; the pottery is Cypriote only by adoption and was made, and enjoyed a widespread popularity on the mainland, long before Cyprus knew anything about it.[1]

At this time there is common in Palestine and the greater part of Syria a very distinctive type of pottery – small jugs of grey or black ware with a decoration of white-filled punctures or incisions – which is generally called Hyksos pottery, associated with the Semitic people who conquered and for a while ruled the Nile delta. We have not found at Atchana more than one doubtfully-related fragment. Level VI did inherit from the preceding period a black lightly-burnished ware, usually in the shape of small jugs, but the typical 'Hyksos' ornament is lacking. Alalakh therefore was not directly affected by that movement and its Palestinian contacts seem to have begun only after the Hyksos had ceased to count – they were driven out of Egypt about 1700 B.C. – i.e. in the latter half of the Level VI period. Throughout that period we can observe development apparently undisturbed by any catastrophe or any marked political change; there is plenty of trade, chiefly with the north and east but, later, with southern countries also, and a few examples of Mycenaean pottery coming in at the close of the period show that the sea routes too were kept open. It was a quiet but not an unprosperous time. It is in Level VI that we find the very finest specimens of Phoenician poly-chrome glass, certainly an expensive luxury, and vases of blue lapis-lazuli paste moulded with figures in relief, which

1. Long ago, when arguing against the view that the 'Cypriote' wares found in such quantities in Level IV were of Cypriote manufacture, I urged that a wholesale trade over land and sea in articles so fragile and so difficult to pack was not an economic proposition, and I must admit that the same holds good for the long overland transit from Anatolia. I am indebted to Professor Mallowan for the suggestion that when imports on a limited scale had established the popularity of the White Slip ware at Alalakh a number of Anatolian craftsmen may have followed in the line of trade and established a working colony in north Syria, importing their raw materials so far as was necessary (this would be easy enough) but making the pots on the spot and keeping to their own technique of hand-made wares instead of adopting the wheel used by the local potters. The same thing may perhaps have happened later in Cyprus.

are as fine as any period could produce. One imported 'luxury article' gave rise to what is perhaps the most curious archaeological incident in my experience; it deserves to be recounted in full.

When we were excavating the courtyard of the Level II temple we suddenly came upon fragments of a blue-glazed earthenware pot. Now the art of glazing objects made of frit, siliceous paste, had been practised since very early days – in Egypt since the First Dynasty period – but the glazing of earthenware is a very different matter, for the glaze will not readily adhere to terra-cotta, and was a much later invention. In Egypt it was not introduced until the Roman age; in Mesopotamia it came earlier – I had myself found several cases of it of the sixth century B.C. – but the earliest known examples were some glazed terra-cotta tiles from the palace of a ninth-century Assyrian king, and archaeologists therefore had agreed that the technique was only discovered early in the first millennium before Christ. An object belonging to Level II at Atchana could not be dated much later than 1300 B.C., which on the available evidence was a quite impossible date for a glazed pot that looked more like an Arab pot of the thirteenth century A.D. I concluded that something was wrong with the stratification and gave my staff a lecture on the importance of not being deceived by appearances – there must have been a rubbish-pit or an animal's burrow or something of the sort which we had failed to notice, and the fragments had infiltered into a wrong level. Shortly afterwards the work brought us down to the brick-paved floor of the court; below where the pottery fragments had been found the pavement was broken up, but close by there was a large patch in good condition. When this had been duly recorded it was lifted, so that the work could go down deeper, and under the undisturbed brickwork we found more fragments of the same pot! This time there could be no doubt about it, and I had to give my staff another lecture to the effect that one mustn't think one knows everything but must approach the work with an unbiased mind open to receive new facts. It was rather humiliating. Some time later we found a complete vase of glazed pottery in a grave belonging to Level V, and afterwards fragments of similar vases occurred in Level VI; to assign a date in the seventeenth century to a glazed earthenware pot was, in a minor way, revolutionary, but it was unavoidable; I was prepared therefore for an archaeological storm.

But when I discussed the matter with Mr C. J. Gadd at the British Museum he referred me to the publication by himself and the late Dr R. Campbell Thompson of a cuneiform tablet in the Museum which dated from the seventeenth century B.C. and was written in the form of a cryptogram, meant to be unintelligible except to the initiate; part of it was frankly unintelligible, concerned, on the face of it, with funeral rites and embryos, but the rest, as translated by the two scholars, was actually a scientific formula for the manufacture of glazed earthenware! Their publication was brought to the notice of Mr H. Moore, who proceeded to submit the formula to a practical test with complete success; – 'As one worked and saw the results coming out as predicted,' he writes, 'one became a profound admirer of that ancient craftsman whose accurate and precise instructions and observations, both as regards quantities and methods, could be followed out some 3600 years later and brought to an immediately successful issue'.[1]

The art of glazing earthenware was therefore learnt by an Assyrian in the seventeenth century B.C. and the secret, carefully protected by its ambiguously-worded description, must have been handed down by the inventor either to his family or to his guild as something not to be divulged to the trade in general; the rarity of the product is explained by the very limited production. It speaks well for the respect accorded to the 'art and mystery' of manufacturing tech-

1. We may admire as profoundly modern scholarship which enabled Messrs Gadd and Thompson to elucidate an Assyrian cryptogram which so long defied Assyrian workers.

nique that this secret was kept for 1000 years! Only in
the seventh century B.C. was the formula published in intelligible language, and from that date the ware becomes
relatively common. Our Atchana examples from Levels VI
and V must be reckoned amongst the earliest products of
the industry – possibly the work of the actual inventor –
and certainly bear witness to the prosperity of Alalakh at
that period when such novelties would naturally command
a very high price.

There is no sign of any violent disaster putting an end to
Level VI; so far as one can see the transition to Level V
involved no more than the erection of new buildings where
old ones had grown unserviceable; nor is there any break
in the cultural sequence; indeed for a long time we had
difficulty in distinguishing the two levels. Professor Sidney
Smith associates the change with the advance of the Anatolian Hittites, 'The pressure southwards continued. Hattusilis
I began the attacks on the territories of Aleppo, Mursilis I
sacked that city in or shortly before 1595; at that time,
presumably, Alalakh fell and Level VI ended. . . . There
were great changes thereafter, but they were not changes
due to Hittite domination, for, once the immediate purpose
of destroying the power of Aleppo and Babylon was accom-
plished, the army of Mursilis retired'. This, I think, we may
fully accept as explaining the occasion of the change. The
destruction of Aleppo would almost certainly be followed
by the fall of Alalakh, but not necessarily by its destruction;
the Hittites had already, as Smith says, obtained their object
and may well have been satisfied to accept its surrender,
perhaps requiring of the citizens that they should dismantle
their fortifications, in which case the building of the earlier
Level V citadel would have been undertaken after the
Hittite withdrawal. With that possible exception we found
no material evidence at Atchana of the Mursilis invasion.

But the period covered by our Level V was not to be so
uniformly quiet as its beginnings seemed to promise. I have
said, when giving reasons for regarding the period as a

long one, that the original Level V citadel had to be rebuilt
during the course of it, and since it was a very solid structure its destruction must have been due to violence and not
merely to time. Now in the little corner of the Level VA
citadel which we cleared – it was only two rooms – we
found a large silo or grain-store and, under the floors, a
number of graves including those of women and children.
The custom of burying people under the floors of their
houses is fairly common in the Middle East though by no
means universal. At Atchana we found no such burials in
the earlier periods; the first occurrence of them is in Level
VIII and they gradually become more common, but even
when they are most numerous, in Level I, they are not
nearly enough to account for the whole population; moreover it is noticeably true that by far the greater proportion
occur in houses of the poorer sort; in the better houses
hardly any (except perhaps infants' burials) are found, and
in the palaces none at all. It is safe to assert that most of the
inhabitants of Alalakh were buried in regular cemeteries
(which we have not discovered) and that only a relatively
small minority adopted, for reasons of religion or economy,
the practice of house burial which in Mesopotamia was at
this time in general use. It is therefore very surprising to
find burials inside the citadel; indeed, this is unique amongst
the public buildings which we have excavated, and there
must have been a special reason for so marked a departure
from the norm. The explanation which I would suggest is
that the people had no choice in the matter, that they buried
their dead in the citadel because they could not bury them
outside, i.e. that there was a siege and Alalakh was 'straitly
shut up, none went out and none came in'; with this the
existence of the grain-pit, also unique so far as our limited
investigations went, would be thoroughly in accord: provisions for the beleaguered garrison had to be stored inside
the fort. In front of the Level V temple we found a number
of rubbish-pits, lying very close together, all made at the
same time – of this we could be sure, for fragments of the

(a) Neolithic stone figurine from the Amq plain

(b) Examples of seals from Tell esh Sheikh

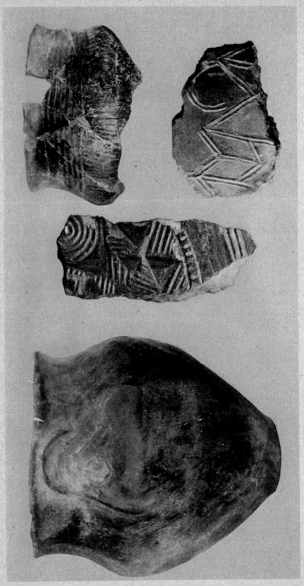

'Khirbet Kerak' pottery from Tabara al Akrad

Examples of early painted pottery from Atchana

The first appearance of the mud-brick columns of the Level XII palace

(*a*) The City Gate of Level VII, looking out over the plain

(*b*) Steps going down to the basalt door of the shaft in the Level VII palace

(a) Specimen of fresco from the Level VII palace

(b) Stone head in Egyptian style from the Level VII temple

Stone head, perhaps a portrait of King Yarim-Lim, from the Level VII temple

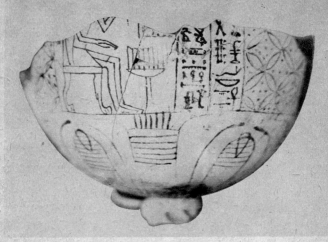

(a) Faience bowl with Egyptian inscription, Level V

(b) Examples of black ware with impressed decoration, Level V

Examples of 'White Slip' and
'Base ring' pottery of the sorts
common to Cyprus

9

(b) Pair of grotesque stone idols from Level V

(a) The 'Mithraeum' with its bench and fire-altar

'Hall of Audience' (room 28) in the Level IV palace, showing half-timber construction: in the hole in the floor is the stone column-base set between two wall-piers

(a) Inscribed statue of King Idri-mi

(b) Entrance of Niqmepa's palace, from the forecourt

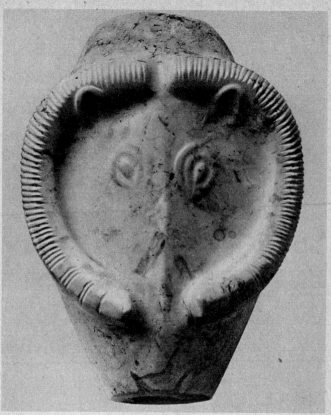

(a) Stone ram's head from the Level IV palace

(b) and (c) Ivory toilet-boxes in the Egyptian style from the Level IV palace

(b) Stone roundel with 'proto-Hittite' inscription

(a) Tablet bearing seal of King Ilim-ilimma: the King carries the Egyptian symbol of long life

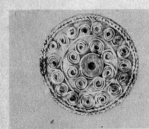

(c) Examples of granulated and filigree work in gold

(d) Clay model of animal's intestines marked to give omens

(a) Hittite relief of the 'Great King' Tudkhalia IV

(b) Store-cellars of the Level III fortress

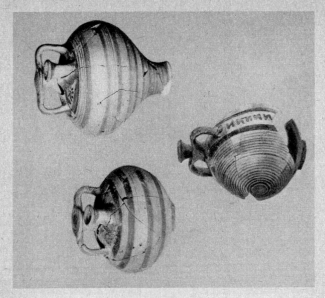

(b) Imported Mycenaean pottery

(a) Goblets with 'Atchana' painted decoration

16

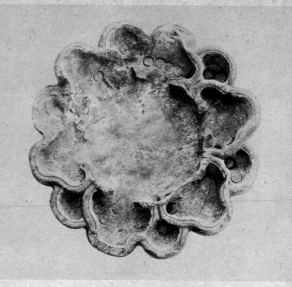

(a) Bronze spearhead with lions, from the Level I temple

(b) Red marble lamp of Cretan style (side and top views)

17

Basalt figures of lions from the Level I temple

(b) Fragments of vases of early Greek island (geometric) ware found at al Mina

(a) Basalt altar from the Level I temple

19

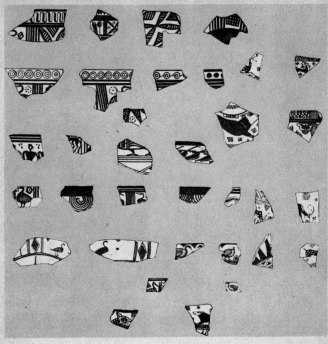

(*a*) Fragments of later Greek island fabrics found at al Mina

(*b*) Cypriote vases from al Mina

(*a*) Attic black-figured kylix from al Mina

(*b*) Attic red-figured vase from al Mina

(a) Attic vases illustrating mass-production methods

(b) Marble head of the City goddess

22

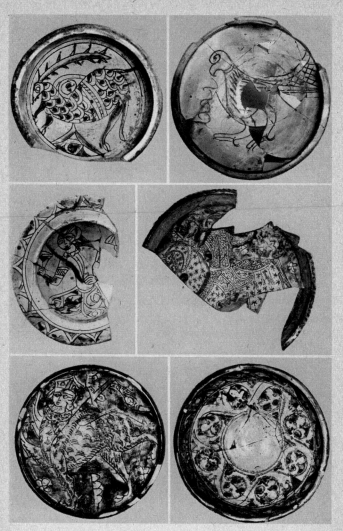

Bowls and fragments of bowls of St Symeon ware

(*a*) View of al Mina from the dried river-bed, showing the eroded cliff; Mount Kasius in the background

(*b*) The monument of 'The Lord of the Sea'

same pottery vessels were found divided between two and
even between three pits – and contemporary with the Level
V temple though at what stage in that existence of the temple
they had been dug it was impossible to say. Judging from
the contents, which included a number of fine examples of
the black pottery with impressed ornament (Pl. 8 b) which
very rarely occurs in private houses, this was a dump of *ex
votos* from the temple, objects which were out of date and no
longer wanted or possibly objects which had been deliberately broken (though we found no evidence of the temple
having been sacked) but, since they had been dedicated to
the gods, could not be treated as mere rubbish and thrown
away outside the sanctuary precincts and so were put into
specially-dug pits on the premises. Amongst them was a
large fragment of a bowl of blue-glazed frit, of Egyptian
manufacture, on which there was drawn in brown paint a
decoration of lotus design and a regular Egyptian scene of
a functionary seated before a table of offerings, with a
hieroglyphic inscription above giving the conventional
dedication-formula; unfortunately the inscription was incomplete and the man's name was lacking, but he calls
himself 'the Scribe', which would be the proper title of a
high official of the Civil Service, a local representative of
the Egyptian Government. If he were indeed anything of
the sort we have here a monument of considerable importance for Egyptian history (Pl. 8 a).

In or about the year 1527 B.C. Thothmes I of Egypt conducted a successful campaign in Syria which ended only on
the Euphrates; he set up trophies on the banks of that river
and he hunted elephants in the land of Niya, part of the old
kingdom of Yamkhad. It has generally been assumed that
this was a mere raid with no political intention or aftermath,
and nothing is said of any capture or surrender of towns,
much less of any attempt to organize them as parts of a
colonial empire. But our sole sources of information about
the campaign are the inscriptions in the tombs of two of
Pharaoh's generals who took a prominent part in it, and all

that they are concerned with is their own prowess – to anything outside their own military exploits they are profoundly indifferent. If the faience bowl from Atchana means what it appears to mean, that there was an Egyptian Resident at Alalakh, then we must suppose that Thothmes I did a great deal more than raid the land of Naharina – the land between the two rivers Euphrates and Orontes – and hunt elephants; he really extended the Egyptian empire. The siege of Alalakh to which the graves in the citadel seem to bear witness may have been an incident in Pharaoh's campaign, and its reduction followed by the installation of an Egyptian governor; something of the sort is implied by the fact that when thirty-five years later Thothmes III invaded north Syria he justified his attack by the plea that the country had rebelled against Egypt. If I have rightly interpreted the Atchana evidence then the credit of having attempted not only the conquest but the colonization of Syria, hitherto assigned to Thothmes III, must go in the first place to his father, Thothmes I.

Egyptian domination however did not last long; the Khurri states of north Syria, amongst which the kingdom of Mitanni was probably already playing a leading part, soon asserted their independence, and at Atchana this is symbolized in a very curious way. Throughout the whole history of Alalakh the record of the city temples is that each was built above the ruins of its predecessor, those ruins often being utilized deliberately to make a raised platform or podium which would give to the new building a more commanding position. To this rule the Level V temple is an extraordinary exception, for the builders, instead of levelling the remains of the Level VI building, dug right through them, making a rectangular pit inside which the new sanctuary was erected; of the Level VI temple only a short stretch of the outer face of the NE. wall escaped utter destruction. The new temple consisted of a court with service-chambers apparently all round it – we found remains of them both on the NE. and on the NW. sides – and the temple proper in the middle; it seems to have had an entrance-chamber at ground level of which all traces have disappeared, but the sanctuary-chamber behind it lay six feet below ground. It was a wide and shallow room measuring twelve foot six from back to front and more than double that across (the SW. end was destroyed by the deep-set foundations of Level IV) and had a broad raised bench along its back and end walls; in the front (SE.) wall was the doorway from the entrance-chamber giving on a flight of wooden steps that lead down to the sunken floor; immediately opposite to them there stood, against the back bench, a fire-altar (Pl. 10 a), a rectangle of plastered brick standing eighteen inches high with in its top a box-like depression that showed marks of heavy burning; on each side of the altar there had been an upright wooden post. As the walls were ruined down to the level of the top of the benches it was impossible to say whether they had been simple or had had niches contrived in the walls' thickness.

In the whole of the Middle East there is no precedent for a temple having its sanctuary sunk below ground level. There is, however, one deity whose shrine regularly took that form, namely Mithras, the eastern god whose worship became so popular with the soldiers of the Roman Empire. But the oldest Mithraeum known to us is not earlier than the second century A.D., after which time the legions built temples to Mithras 'also a soldier' wherever they might be stationed, from Northumberland to Austria, and the ruins of these, with benches, flight of steps and fire-altar, are sometimes remarkably like ours at Atchana. Since there is nothing to bridge the time gap it would seem rash indeed to argue from a Roman building of the second or third century A.D. to one in Syria of the sixteenth or early fifteenth century B.C.; but Mithras is an Indo-European god, and we have to remember that just at this time the kingdom of Mitanni was the chief power in north Syria and the rulers of that kingdom were immigrants of an Indo-European stock who did in fact introduce the Indo-European gods into Asia, so much so that in their treaties they will invoke Mithras as a witness to their good faith. If Alalakh made common cause with Mitanni it was almost inevitable, by the practice of the ancient East, that it should pay to the stronger Power the compliment of adopting its religion or, at any rate, of adding one of its gods to the local pantheon.[1] The theory that the peculiar Atchana temple is a Mithraeum (by far the earliest known) agrees so well with the political conditions then prevailing that it should be accepted; the people of Alalakh, joining in the general rebellion against Egypt, naturally put themselves under the aegis of their strongest neighbour.

Further discoveries threw more light on the religious attitude of the period. When we were excavating the private houses of Level IV we came upon the ruins of a small building which I at first took to belong to that level; later, finding that part of it had been destroyed to make room for an addition to a Level IV house, I was able to fix its date more exactly and assign it to the second half of the Level V period with an overlap into Level IV. The building was a small one-room shrine set on a low brick-faced platform with sloped clay-plastered glacis sides above which rose a brick parapet-wall; the shrine itself had very solid walls, four feet thick, with lower courses of limestone blocks and mud-brick above, and a wide doorway with stone jambs and threshold; the interior, only six and a half feet wide (its length is unknown because the SW. end was never found) was paved with stone slabs and the wall face was neatly rendered with white lime plaster; by the door was found a small gold crescent pendant and close by was the cult object, a triangular-shaped slab of undressed stone, quite rough, but having on one side a very crude sketch of a human face. Six feet away to the NW. there was part of a precisely similar platform; only a thirty-foot stretch of one

1. This is the explanation of Solomon's building at Jerusalem temples to Astarte (as a compliment to his ally Hiram of Tyre) and to an Egyptian deity, as a symbol of his subjection to Pharaoh.

wall survived, with nothing at all of the superstructure, but it would appear that there had been two shrines side by side, presumably for the worship of twin deities.

Considering that Level V was quite a sophisticated period we were surprised to find belonging to it so crude a representation of a god; but two or three equally crude stone figurines occurred in house sites of the same level and a larger pair discovered by accident furnished us with an explanation. In 1939 we had excavated the town gateway of Level VII and having come first on the inner pair of piers had been able to clear the whole of the entrance, following the stone facing-slabs of the walls and leaving untouched above them the original brickwork so far as it was preserved and on the top of the brickwork the accumulated rubbish of subsequent centuries which, trimmed by us to a straight face, gave for the time being a very good impression of upstanding walls. During the war a winter's rain loosened the soil and a big slice of our imitation wall collapsed, exposing in the new rubbish face two basalt statues, male and female, standing in position in a chamber adjoining the Level V town gate (Pl. 10 b). As works of art they were grotesquely, almost obscenely bad, but they proved most instructive. Mr Ahmet Dönmes, who was assisting me in the excavations, drew my attention to a pair of basalt figures found in one of the gateways of Diyarbakir; the male figure there differed in that he had a beard, but was in the same style, while the female figure was a twin sister of the Alalakh goddess. Now Diyarbakir is a city in the middle of the Mitanni country, and the connexion therefore becomes obvious; Alalakh, attaching itself to the Mitanni confederation, naturally adopts the worship of a people artistically inferior but politically pre-eminent.

On the other hand the social life of the city was relatively undisturbed by the political changes; the objects which we found in the houses and in the graves of the period show for the most part a straightforward development of the culture of Level VI. The so-called 'Cypriote' pottery be-

comes more common, the painted Palestinian ware characteristic of the later phase of the previous period continues
in use; there is really only one novelty which is peculiar to
the level. This is a striking type of pottery, black in colour,
burnished and decorated with geometrical patterns in white
made by impressing in the soft clay lines and circles done
with chisel-shaped tools of varying sizes and with tubes,
perhaps sections of reeds, and then filling in the impressions
with white paste; the technique is evidently borrowed from
workers in metal, and the shapes of the vessels (only two
shapes occur) are likewise metallic (Pl. 8 b). The pottery
is not local in that it has no antecedents at Atchana and
after enjoying a brief vogue there goes right out of use, and
we do not yet know where it originated, but examples
(of a different shape) have been found at Tarsus in Cilicia
and a somewhat similar but not identical ware occurs at
about this time in northern Mesopotamia. Since our best
specimens were found in the rubbish-pits of the Level V
temple in which the Egyptian bowl also was found we may
assume that the ware was introduced fairly early in the
period, but it does occur in later houses also. Probably
therefore the importation of this black impressed ware
means that the association of Alalakh with the north Syrian
states further to the east, which can be traced in Level VI,
continued in the Level V period and was not seriously interrupted by the short Egyptian domination; the latter might
involve the dismantling of the town fortifications (if those
had not already been destroyed as a result of the siege) but
did not greatly affect the lives of the ordinary citizens and
the trade of the merchants.

So far as the monuments on the site are concerned there
is a certain vagueness in the distinction between Levels V
and IV. Our archaeological Level IV starts with the founding of the royal palace which is the outstanding building of
the period, contrasts with all the rest in its different orientation, and can fairly be considered to mark the beginning of a
new era. But the palace itself does incorporate parts of an

older structure, and there are other public buildings which in their use are contemporary with the palace but in their foundation considerably earlier; they had, in fact, been put up in the latter part of the Level V period and survived well into the period of Level IV. Just as there is an overlap of the buildings so there is of social and political conditions; the erection of a new palace signalizes the emergence of a new régime, which we can properly call Level IV, but the foundations of that régime go back into Level V and were laid by a major event of the period.

Thothmes III of Egypt was, during all the early part of his reign, hard put to it to establish his power against the machinations of his half-sister, Queen Hatshepsut; indeed it was this preoccupation that made possible the revolt of Syria. When, after twenty years, her death secured his freedom of action, the Pharaoh started on a methodical campaign of reconquest; he gradually subdued the south, in the year 1488 B.C. he crossed the Euphrates and successfully attacked the suzerain power, Mitanni 'that contemptible enemy', and in 1483 B.C. he was receiving the tribute of Alalakh whose formal surrender must have taken place a year or so earlier. Thothmes III was aiming at empire and his methods therefore were those of organization, not of destruction; we need not expect to find, and we do not find, any sign of damage to our city, which had probably given in as soon as the capture of Niya proved the uselessness of resistance. On the contrary, I suspect that those public buildings which date from the latter part of the period and survive far into the next are the work of the régime instituted or supported and confirmed by the Pharaoh. Their continuity accords with the historical facts as we understand them from such literary documents as exist.[1] According to them, Thothmes III reorganized the position in north Syria, grouping together several minor kingdoms under the

1. I am accepting here Sidney Smith's view of the Amarna letter No. 51, written by Adad-nirari, whom he identifies with Adad-nirari, son of Idri-mi; see later, p. 136.

name of Nuḥašši and setting over them Taku, the founder of the dynasty which was to rule Alalakh for the next hundred years. It is likely that Taku was already king of Alalakh, but as the vassal of Egypt he ruled a much wider domain, extending from the Euphrates to the Mediterranean and from the northern edge of the Amq plain southwards through Nuḥašši to the neighbourhood of Apamea; it was a rather loose conglomeration not likely to be too stable (Thothmes himself seems to have anticipated trouble, judging by the phrasing of the order which set Taku on the throne) but for the moment at least it was guaranteed by the power of Egypt and its ruler was a man of consequence; he would almost certainly signalize his aggrandizement by the erection of new public buildings in his capital, and it is only natural that his lineal descendants should have continued to use them. Taku then, and his immediate successors, fall within the limits of our archaeological Level V, and Level IV begins with the accession of Niqmepa.

CHAPTER VII

The Niqmepa Dynasty

Level IV

*

OUR archaeological Level IV begins a little before 1450 and ends about 1370 B.C. and is far more fully documented than any other period. On the literary side we have a mass of inscribed tablets found in the royal palace and the auto-biography of king Idri-mi inscribed on his statue; the archaeological material includes the whole of the palace, remarkably well preserved, remains of the temple, a large area inside the citadel, the town gate with its surrounding buildings, a number of private houses, and rather more than forty graves[1] containing pottery and other objects; the palace produced, besides tablets, a quite astonishing amount of pottery and objects in ivory and metal.

Since the great majority of the tablets belong to the reign of king Niqmepa and none of them are earlier, the building of the palace in which they were kept can safely be assigned to him. The site which he chose was that of an earlier palace, probably erected in the time of Level V and retained in use by the first kings of Niqmepa's house who owed their throne to Thothmes III of Egypt, and he himself preserved the greater part of it, simply adding a new residential block for the use of the royal family at the cost of the destruction of a few rooms of the old building and the sacrifice of the east side of the 'parade-ground' which lay inside the city

1. Seventeen of them were dated to the period by their association with the houses; twenty-five were dated by internal evidence, i.e. by the pottery types found in them.

gate and in front of the citadel façade. But for some inexplicable reason he orientated his new work quite differently from the old; it cuts across the lines of the old walls at an incongruous angle, and the forecourt of the palace,

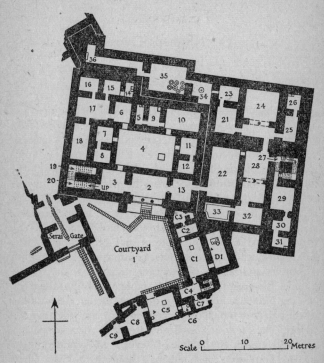

Fig. 14. *Plan of the Palace of Level IV*

bounded on two sides by the domestic quarters of the former palace and on a third by the back wall of the citadel entrance-gate erected in the Level V period is so irregular that the imposing front of the palace loses much of its effect. At a later period, perhaps in the reign of Ilim-ilimma, Niqmepa's son, the size of the new palace was about doubled by the addition of a range of chambers outside its north wall and of a complete block against the east wall; for the construction of the latter all that had remained of the main building of the Level V palace was swept away, leaving only the old kitchen wing fronting on the courtyard, and the eastern block was orientated to match Niqmepa's residence; judging from the character of the building we can say that Ilim-ilimma was completing his father's work by adding to the residential quarters an 'official' wing for the transaction of public business. The plan on Fig. 14, p. 106, shows the royal palace as it was in Ilim-ilimma's time, i.e. in its final form; on it the pre-Niqmepa rooms are distinguished by the letters C and D with the room number; under Ilim-ilimma's courtyard (21) we found parts of the wall and concrete floor of the original Level V palace re-used by Niqmepa, but those were too fragmentary to be shown. In its ground-plan Niqmepa's building is really an enlarged version of the better-class private house of the period, consisting essentially of a series of rooms ranged round a central court (4); Ilim-ilimma's wing is on the contrary entirely given over to 'chambers of audience' such as we saw in Yarim-Lim's palace and to subordinate offices; the chambers of audience are central and the light-well or court (21) is on one side of the building.

As one entered the forecourt of the palace by the main gateway in its western wall the skew buildings on one's right and in front were all that was left of the Level V palace; their character was amply demonstrated by the contents of the rooms. In the larger rooms (C1, C5, D1) there were hearths, ovens, and tripods on which the cooking-pots were stood over the fires, grindstones and pestles, stone mortars, and all the paraphernalia of the kitchen; fireproof cooking-pots were strewn about the floors, and in the smaller rooms there were quantities of domestic pottery evidently kept in store there; a tiny cellar-like room (C6) was largely taken up by a huge store-vase let into its floor. A small staircase (in room C4) showed that there had been an upper storey, and one may suppose that the kitchen staff slept in the upstairs rooms. As all the food must have been prepared in this wing and carried to the palace proper a path of terra-cotta tiles was laid along the courtyard wall from the kitchens to the palace entrance, a wise provision against the slippery mud of a North Syrian winter; a similar narrow tiled path led to the entrance from a small door in the NW. corner of the court; this opened into one of the door-recesses of the great gateway of the citadel and was probably for the use of the soldiers detailed for guard duty at the palace.

The palace entrance (Fl. 12 b) was a very striking architectural feature. Between two buttresses which probably supported a balcony there was a flight of three basalt steps flanked by flat-topped platforms faced with polished slabs of basalt set in cement; at the head of the steps, on the level of the tops of the platforms, was the limestone sill of a doorway twenty-six feet wide, the total span divided by two wooden columns whose bases were drums of polished basalt; the jambs of the doorway and the walls of the room beyond were lined with three-foot-high basalt slabs resting on a course of limestone blocks masked by a chamfered skirting of fine white cement; above the stones the walls were carried up in half-timber construction. The building-methods used are indeed those which were traditional in the country, and even the details of the plan have much in common with the Yarim-Lim palace of three centuries before; the architecture is native, developed in Asia, and when we find parallels in other lands they are due to those lands borrowing ideas from Asia and not *vice versa*. And such parallels do exist. When in 1937 we unearthed just this part of the palace – the steps with their flanking platforms and the entrance-chamber, we found a solid mass of mud brick-work running across from one door-jamb to the other; it was not easy to get a true wall-face, but since the bricks were not loose but firmly compacted with their mud mortar we could only conclude that this was a wall, and a wall *in situ*, although its surface had suffered badly and although it seemed anomalous in that it blocked the head of the steps. Suddenly it struck me that the whole thing had a remarkably Cretan appearance, but in Crete there would have been at the top of the steps two columns with a door opening between them; accordingly I marked out two circles and told the workmen to dig away the brickwork there, and when they looked scandalized at the idea of destroying a standing wall said that they would find in each marked spot a stone column-base. They dug, and the stone column-bases duly appeared, set on the limestone threshold which had been hidden hitherto; our 'wall' was indeed a wall, but it was that of the upper storey which with the burning of the wooden architrave above the columns had fallen down into a coherent mass on the threshold. I think that the story illustrates better than anything else the close analogy between Alalakh and Knossos.

The only entrance to the palace was by the steps from the courtyard, and the entrance-chamber must have served as the guardroom; a door on the right led to a lobby through which one passed to the official wing, and a door on the left led to another lobby (3), off which opened the palace staircase (19–20) and a second door giving access to the central court. The court, cement-paved and having a raised hearth for an open-air fire (a usual feature), was symmetrically laid out with four doors leading to the various rooms, thirteen in all, on the ground floor. As in Yarim-Lim's palace, so here the best rooms, the king's suite, were in the upper storey, but considering that there was a good deal of accommodation for the staff in and above the kitchen wing we cannot say that the whole of the ground-floor of the palace proper was given over to the domestics; on the contrary, while there are four rooms, 7 and 8, and 11 and 12, which may quite well have been servants' quarters, all the rest are grouped in two self-contained flats of different sizes and the arrangement suggests that they were the residences either of important court functionaries or of junior members of the royal family. Thus in the group 10, 9 and 5, room 5, with cemented floor and walls, is a lavatory precisely of the sort used in the Middle East at the present time; the out-flow drain of terra-cotta pipes went down and under the wall and must have been taken through the city wall (we could not follow it there) to empty on the glacis; room 9, also cement-plastered, was a bathroom with a big terra-cotta bath let into the floor in one corner; room 10, with no particular features, may have been a bedroom but it did contain a number of tablets. In the larger group we have a lavatory in the little room 14; room 15, having cemented walls, was a bathroom though no fixed bath was found in it. Room 18 produced nothing, but the rooms 6, 16 and 17 were filled with pottery which had obviously been stored there in bulk; there were hundreds of large plates often still in piles of ten or a dozen, the slant of the piles showing that they had slipped down from wooden shelves arranged along the walls, and scores of jugs of the fine biscuit clay that in Cyprus is called 'Base-Ring Ware' and of the white milk-bowls with ladder-like decoration in black and red; there were fancy jugs in the form of cows, of grey clay with details painted in white, and jugs of local ware some of which, like the plates, were burnished or decorated with concentric circles of red paint; we had before us the complete crockery outfit of the royal palace. Incongruously mixed with the pottery were numerous ob-jects of a very different kind which had certainly fallen from the rooms above when the floors collapsed at the time of the building's destruction; amongst them were ivory toilet-boxes of Egyptian design (but almost certainly of local make), three in the form of seated ducks, one with a woman's head wearing the Egyptian head-dress (Pl. 13 b and c), and a large spherical gold bead of cloisonné work, inlaid with lapis lazuli and white shell in the old Sumerian style; in the courtyard we had found two fragments of gold binding for a staff decorated with a pattern of triangles in very fine granulated technique closely resembling Aegean work (cf. Pl. 14 c), so that the international character of the luxury objects in the palace was well represented. In room 18, above the ashes of the ceiling-beams and therefore belonging to an upper room, there were hundreds of fragments of narrow gold strip and of ivory in squares, circles, diamonds, and triangles; these were for inlay in furniture of a sort very much like that made at the present day in Damascus where the bazaars are filled with stools and tablets incrusted with similar shapes in mother-of-pearl and bands of brass wire. In one of the Level IV private houses we found a bit of strip ivory semicircular in section and cut diagonally at each end; it was a piece of inlay from furniture in which an edging in relief is made up of alternate lengths of ivory and dark wood cut so as to give the effect of a twisted cord; precisely that decoration, made in the same way, appears on a chest of drawers in my possession which was manufactured in Turkey in the late eighteenth century. Naturally we cannot expect to find any wooden objects surviving in the soil of North Syria, and it is fortunate that these ivory fragments, valueless in themselves, enable us, thanks to the conservatism of the Middle East, to picture with tolerable accuracy the furnishing of a royal palace of the fifteenth century B.C. Two small column-bases of basalt which had fallen from the upper rooms showed that in the royal apartments one room at least had been a saloon of the 'hall of audience' type, as was the case in Yarim-Lim's palace also; this is suggested in Mr Lavers' restored plan on Fig. 15.

In the new wing, which we suppose to have been added by Ilim-ilimma, the same methods of construction were used as in the older part of the palace – the dado of polished basalt slabs, the half-timberwork of the walls, and the white cement for floors; judging by the unusual thickness of some of the walls part of the building at least was three storeys high. The main block falls into two more or less identical sections; at the northern end room 14 is a 'hall of audience' divided by the normal buttresses and a single column, having on one side of it a retiring-room and a lavatory (26) and on the other two rooms which may have composed the secretariat; in the southern section room 28 (Pl. 11) is again a 'hall of audience' having on one side, beyond the staircase, two rooms and a lavatory (31) and behind it (since on its other side was the open court, 21) the secretary's office and opening off that the archive, room 33, a small room which had a low brick shelf running all round it. As soon as we saw the shelf we could guess the nature of the room since we had found one exactly like it at Ur, and there numerous tablets had been found lying on the shelves; in this case the shelves had been swept clean, much to our disappointment, but as soon as we dug down in the middle of the room the expected tablets were duly forthcoming, scattered all about the floor.

The staircase in room 27 was of the traditional type with a central newel of half-timber construction, the two lower flights having wooden treads over a solid packing and the third flight supported by timber joists with a cupboard beneath. Ilim-ilimma's further addition, on the north side of the palace, was purely domestic; the main room (35) served as a cellar and was filled with great store-jars partly sunk in the floor – some of them were found almost intact – and the adjoining room 34 had a cement floor sloping down to a central drain, which suggested that it had been used for some such operation as the decanting of the oil or wine stored in the jars. The long passage leading to the tiny room 36 (in which some tablets were found) was too ruined for anything more than its ground-plan to be recognizable, but it may have led to a staircase in what was certainly a very solid tower forming the corner of the building.

The official character of this block was emphasized by the fact that practically nothing was found in it – there was scarcely a single clay pot in the whole building, a marked contrast to the conditions in the residential block. The only object, apart from numerous tablets, was a white limestone head of a ram found in room 29, into which it had fallen.

The head (Pl. 13 a), just over a foot high, is pierced verti-
cally as if it were a spout (though what purpose it actually
served one cannot know) and the top of the head has been

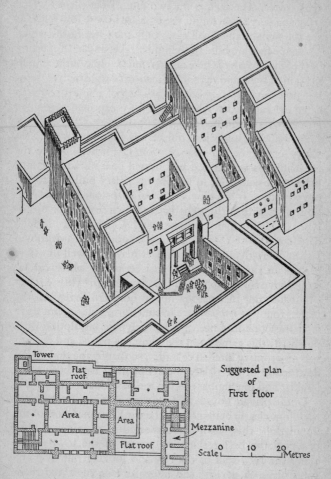

Fig. 15. *Restored Elevation of the Palace of Level IV*

left rough, implying that it either fitted into or was covered by something in a different material. In any case it is a piece of applied decoration, but as a work of art it is indeed remarkable. The face is on two almost flat planes which meet at a very slight angle, the eyes are in very low relief, as are the unnaturally small ears; only the great horns which frame the face are bold both in their relief and in the cutting of the rings. We have here an extreme example of the simplification of form and the subordination of realism to pattern; it is no primitive essay but the product of a highly sophisticated art such as we should not have expected to find in North Syria at this period.

A small but important object was found in the kitchen wing, just below the floor of room C3; it belonged to the pre-Niqmepa period and was buried beneath an awkward brickwork patch put in to join his palace building to the old structure. It is a circular seal of soapstone inscribed on both sides with curious characters which seem to be prototypes of Hittite hieroglyphic signs (Pl. 14 b); since it must date from before 1450 B.C., which is earlier than any known Hittite hieroglyphic inscription, it may very well illustrate a stage in the formation of that script, in which case it would give some support to the view that the Hittite script originated not in Anatolia but in northern Syria. All the tablets found at Atchana are in cuneiform writing, but there is at least one instance of a hieroglyphic inscription on a potsherd; this came from the Niqmepa palace and the pot was an ordinary kitchen colander, so that by the time of the destruction of the palace the script must have been fairly familiar and intelligible even to the less educated class.

Of the private houses that we excavated most were large buildings clearly belonging to the wealthier members of the population; this was to be expected in as much as they occupied the best residential quarter of the town, lying along the NE. wall of the city and looking out over the Amq plain. A narrow and irregular lane separated them from the city wall, and at intervals between the houses there were other lanes, at right angles to it, leading off into the interior of the town. All the houses were two storeys high and the rooms were arranged round three or all the sides of a central court or light-well off which they opened either directly or through neighbouring rooms. The walls, generally fairly thick, were of brick only with, so far as we could see, no timber built into the brick courses, and though the foundations were as a rule of rough stone rubble no stone was used above-ground; in one house the front door – an exceptionally wide one, possibly provided with a central column – had door-jambs of polished basalt, but there was not a single case of the stone dado such as is habitual in temples and in royal palaces; as if to compensate for this the only room of which any of the wall decoration remained was frescoed with an 'architectural' design reproducing in paint the constructional features of a palace – basalt dado and half-timber work above, the beams coloured red with graining in blue-black, the brick surface plain white. Certainly not many of the ground-floor rooms had been so treated, for most of them apparently had served too utilitarian purposes; each house had one or two lavatories – the fact of their lying close to the city wall made sanitation easy, the pipes running under the lane and through the foundations of the ramparts – and there was always one room which oven and hearth designated as a kitchen, while a thickly cemented floor was probable evidence for a bathroom; but in several cases where the use of the room could not be guessed a plain coat of whitewash over the mud plaster of the wall showed that it had not been one calling for display or justifying expense; probably, in the private house as in the palace, the better rooms were upstairs and the ground-floor was given up for the most part to domestic needs. In one house a stone column-base fallen from an upper room implied that such might possess architectural features recalling the 'hall of audience'; one can only repeat that Niqmepa's residential block is really but an enlarged version of the better-class private house of the period. Of the smaller houses such remains as we found were too fragmentary to give a ground-plan, but with their little box-like rooms and thin walls they were evidently one-storey buildings – probably with flat roofs which could be used for sitting out or for sleeping on in hot weather – crowded closely together and with scanty accommodation inside. What was important about them was the fact that numerous graves were found under their floors, which in the big houses was seldom if ever the case; apparently the richer inhabitants of Alalakh were buried in regular cemeteries outside the city walls whereas the poor, unable to afford the graveyard fees, laid their dead beneath the floors of their own houses or in the little courtyards attached to them. The graves were of the simplest sort. There were no coffins,[1] but the body, clothed, was laid in the earth on one side, the hands before the face, the knees drawn up slightly in the attitude of one asleep; by the shoulder we would find one or two pins that had fastened the cloak, there would be finger-rings and perhaps a cylinder seal and, with the women, beads and amulets at the neck, with children knuckle-bones or, rarely, a clay doll. Apart from such personal possessions there were the offerings made to the dead, a few clay pots for the food and drink required, and that was all. Curiously enough there were never any weapons; either soldiers were buried elsewhere, or the world to which they were going was one in which there was no need of arms. There was no rule of orientation – the heads might be towards any point of the compass in-discriminately, which implies a certain vagueness of religious belief – and the habit of burying under the house floor has none of that religious significance which it had in Mesopo-tamia after the time of the Third Dynasty of Ur when its intention was to preserve the unity of the family; here the sole reason seems to be economical. Infants were buried unceremoniously in clay jars for which but a shallow hole would be dug wherever it was convenient to do so – again,

1. The only wooden coffin found belonged to Level V.

there was no ritual about it, but in these pot-burials the bones were unburnt: cremation was a custom still foreign to Alalakh.

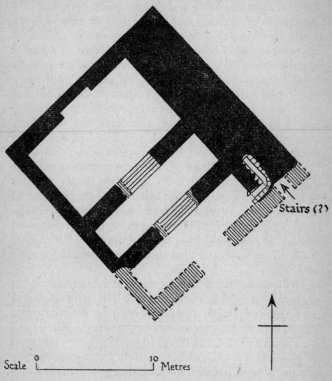

Stairs (?)

Scale 0 ⎣_____⎦ 10 Metres

Fig. 16. *Level IV Temple Plan*

It was almost inevitable that under the Niqmepa dynasty the city temple should be reconstructed, and that was indeed done, but the building was found by us in too ruinous a state for much to be said about it. It consisted of an entrance-chamber, wide and shallow, with apparently an open porch in front of it; the unusually wide doorway is central, and corresponding to it in the back wall is the doorway of the sanctuary proper, and in the back wall of that a deep niche as if for a statue. The comparative thinness of the walls shows that the building was of one storey only, but it is likely that the sanctuary was higher than the antechamber; a staircase on one side led to the flat roof of either room; in that case it would bear a partial resemblance to a model found at Baisan in Palestine, but this is not sufficient grounds for identifying the type of worship favoured by the dynasty of the time. All that we can assert is that the cult of Mithras which we thought we could distinguish in the preceding period had in Level IV been abandoned for something quite different, presumably one which would not by its Mitanni character offend the Pharaoh to whom the ruling family owed its position and, when circumstances required it, professed its devotion. So far as the scanty remains allowed us to judge, the foundation of the temple dated to early in Level IV and its fabric underwent no change throughout the period; it escaped the fire which destroyed Niqmepa's palace and lived on until the Level III builders cut down its walls and used them as foundations for their own work.

To the west of the royal palace stretched the great complex of buildings which comprised the NE. city gate and the fortress or citadel. All of these are older than the palace which, with its different orientation, upsets the planning of the eastern side of the gateway; all must have been inherited by Niqmepa from his forebears and they were preserved by him unchanged; but after his time, though still in the Level IV period, drastic alterations were made in the interior of the citadel. Of those I shall speak later.

The city gate shows a wholly different conception of military defences from that which modelled the gateway of Level VII. A small tower, only about twenty-three feet in either direction and projecting only three feet from the line of the wall, was pierced by a six-foot wide opening secured by a single door set not between piers but directly against the side walls; immediately inside the tower the entrance-passage made a double right-angled turn and then ran on for about fifteen yards between one-storey buildings to debouch on the 'parade-ground' lying in front of the citadel.

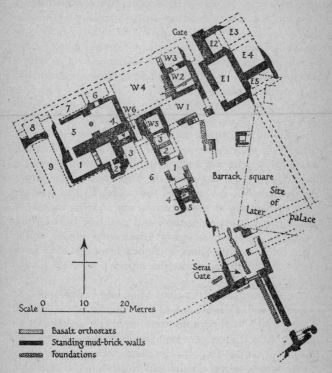

Fig. 17. *Plan of the Citadel and NE. Town Gate of Level IV*

Yarim-Lim's great three-gated tower had failed to keep out an enemy (perhaps because of the weakness inherent in its plan which we have already noted) and the Level V builders had adopted both here and in the SW. gate of the town a new system in which men were to count more than bricks and wood. Should the attackers succeed in bursting through the one doorway their rush would be checked by the blank wall facing them; slowed down by the double turn they would have to advance in a cramped space, exposed all the time to the fire of defenders manning the roofs on either side, and at last would emerge from the passage, not more than three abreast (it widened only to eight feet) to meet the whole main force of the garrison deployed freely on the parade-ground. While not nearly so imposing a structure, the new gateway was far more scientifically designed than that which it replaced.

According to the original plan the parade-ground had been a rectangle measuring rather more than thirty yards by twenty, but Niqmepa's palace, encroaching on it, had reduced it to an irregular triangle. At the south end of this was a triple gateway leading into the town proper; the west side of the triangle was the blank wall of the palace, the east side was the façade of the citadel. By this arrangement the military area was entirely cut off from the rest of the city; it formed an enclave and could be held against civic rebellion as well as against attack from outside, and in peace time when the gates were open anyone passing in or out of the city did so under the supervision of the citadel guard.

The greater part of the citadel building had disappeared as a result of the denudation of the mound's summit, but in the NE. section conditions were more favourable and although the walls were not standing more than a foot above floor level yet the details of the rooms were perfectly clear.

The façade facing on the parade-ground was a double wall with intramural chambers of no great size; in the centre was the entrance, its two doorways, set not quite in line, dignified by fine basalt jambs; this led into an inner court measuring about fourteen yards from NW. to SE. (its SW. limit could not be found) surrounded by the fortress buildings. When we excavated the range on the NW. side of the court we were somewhat surprised, knowing that we were working on a fortress site, to come upon two large rooms of the 'hall of audience' type lying side by side, communicating with each other and each provided with the subsidiary chambers associated with the 'halls of audience' in the royal palaces. Various constructional features – walls plastered one against another, breaks in bond, etc. – made it obvious that the two rooms were not of the same date; one was apparently original to the building, i.e. was a Level V foundation, the other had been added considerably later, and its addition implied a complete remodelling of this part of the citadel. The change had not been due to the destruction of the old building – at least there was no sign of anything of the sort – but must have been the adaptation of the building to a new purpose; when this was done we could not determine with certainty, but it was in the Level IV period, and it was tempting to connect it with another change whereby the level of the parade-ground was raised and (so far as we could make out, but the evidence was none too good) its floor carried over the burnt ruins of Niqmepa's palace. In the end the citadel too was burnt, but it was quite certain that this had nothing to do with the conflagration which destroyed the palace but occurred at a much later date, in fact, at the time when Level IV ended and Level III took its place; the walls of the Level III fort come immediately above the ruins of the Level IV citadel, but where those walls run on over the Niqmepa palace they are separated from it by an intermediate floor-level laid above the burnt ruins, the floor which I believe to be contemporary with the remodelling of the citadel.

This fact has an important bearing on the history of the period. It is a time unusually well documented, for besides the hundreds of tablets found both in the palace and in the rooms at the NW end of the parade-ground (one of which seems to have served as an administrative office for a palace functionary) we have the unique record contained in the autobiography of King Idri-mi. But before dealing with the history I must give an account of this, the outstanding object connected with Level IV.

When we excavated the Level I temple, which was destroyed in 1194 B.C. by the great invasion of the Peoples of the Sea, we found its forecourt littered with objects belonging to the final phase of the building; amongst them was a much defaced basalt throne, obviously that of a statue. In a room in the annexe of the temple proper, lying NE. of the court, we found a hole which had been dug into the floor and filled with earth and large stones (the largest weighing nearly a ton and a half) and smoothed over; under the stones there was a broken statue; the head, which had been knocked off, was set beside the body together with two smaller fragments, one of the beard, the other of a foot; only part of one foot was missing. The statue belonged to the throne found on the temple floor, for it fitted exactly into the cut socket and, besides, there is no detail carved on those parts of the figure which would be hidden by the arms of the throne. We can be sure that the statue was on its throne when the temple was destroyed because the breaking of the feet must have resulted from its being knocked violently off its base into which the feet were socketted; probably the same blow broke the head off from the body. After the sack of the temple someone must have crept back and piously collected all that he could find of the figure and hidden it in a hastily-dug hole in the hope of recovering it later. But the whole city of Alalakh had perished utterly and never recovered; the man who had so cared for Idri-mi never came back; the fallen brickwork of the temple walls buried out of sight the objects strewn about its floor and no man knew of them or sought them out until we dug there in 1939. An interesting point is that the statue dates to about 1400 B.C. and had been preserved in the temple for 200 years and even after that lapse of time was so venerated that a man risked his life to salve it. The king whom the statue represents was not at all so great and successful a ruler as to command such devotion, and I am inclined to think that the statue was prized for its own sake. True, as a work of art it possesses little merit – frankly, it is comically hideous (Pl. 12 a) – but it is at least indigenous, owing nothing to Egypt or Mesopotamia or any other centre known to us; with the single exception of the ram's head found in Niqmepa's palace, which should antedate it by not more than thirty years, it is the oldest piece of sculpture from Alalakh; our evidence tends to show that the whole school of North Syrian art which in later times was to produce the sculptured decoration of the Syro-Hittite palaces took its rise just about this time – in the fifteenth or early fourteenth century – and it is possible that Alalakh treasured our statue not as a portrait but as a 'primitive', the oldest surviving monument of the local school of art.

The figure is carved in fine white magnesite. It was roughed out with a tubular drill and then smoothed down with a grinder and polished. The king is represented as sitting, wrapped in a shapeless garment which has no folds and does not in any way adapt itself to the form of the body; it is a solid casing, and though it suggests an under tunic and a fringed cloak it is so schematized as to bear no relation to any actual clothes. He wears a high conical head-dress, plain and smooth, confined by a simple bandeau; his whiskers and long beard are equally plain; his eyebrows and eyes are inlaid with black stone which is in startling contrast to the extreme whiteness of the magnesite, but no doubt there was originally a free use of paint – a king's beard, for instance, should be elaborately curled, and since here the stone is not worked such detail must have been rendered in colour. The whole front of the figure, from the cheek to the skirts of the clothing, is covered by a cunei-form inscription in 104 lines.

The throne was in the form of a chair having a high back and arms supported by figures of lions, their bodies carved in relief, their heads projecting; there seems to have been a flight of steps in front of the throne, but that was made in a separate block and has been broken away and lost.

The inscription is an autobiography of the king. It was written by a scribe named Sharruwa who may have been one of the 'elder statesmen' of the kingdom, for his name appears on a document of an earlier reign, and here the way in which he speaks of himself and invokes blessings on his own head is a piece of self-assertion that could only have been excused by very high rank. Sharruwa wrote in his own dialect, possibly with some deliberate archaisms; unfortunately neither the scribe who made the copy for the mason nor the mason who cut the inscription was very skilful, and the text is therefore unusually difficult to read. Mr Sidney Smith, who published the document, anticipated that many corrections in the text would be necessary, and there have been differences of opinion on a number of points, the most serious of which calls in question the actual date of Idri-mi's reign, whether, that is, it preceded or followed that of Niqmepa. This depends partly upon the reading adopted for one name in the inscription,[1] partly upon the identity of individuals; in the royal family of Alalakh, as of other Syrian states, names tended to reappear in different generations, so that Niqmepa is the son of Idri-mi and father of Ilim-ilimma, while king Idri-mi is the son of Ilim-ilimma, and accordingly as one chooses to identify the two Idri-mis or the two Ilim-ilimmas the author of our inscription becomes the father or the grandson of the builder of our palace. The philological field is one on which only the linguistic expert can play, but in the historical issue at stake the archaeological evidence must be given due weight, and the archaeological evidence is emphatically and, I think, overwhelmingly in favour of Idri-mi being later in date than Niqmepa. As an archaeologist therefore I have no hesitation in following the lead of Sidney Smith (who has himself argued for the historical justification of his views) and shall

1. Sidney Smith reads it as Shutarna, King of Mitanni; others suggest Ba-ra-at-tar-na which, with a certain amount of manipulation of the signs, might become Par-sa-sha-tar, the father of Shaushshatar, an earlier Mitanni king.

sketch the history of Level IV without further reference to the linguistic arguments of his opponents.

When Thothmes III established in authority Taku, the founder of the Niqmepa dynasty, he seems to have made him overlord of a wider territory than his predecessors had ruled. Alalakh was the capital of the kingdom of Mukishe, which comprised at least the northern part of the Amq plain and stretched westwards, following the course of the lower Orontes, to the shores of the Mediterranean; with this went Ama'u, apparently the rough hill country south of the Plain; the kingdom of Aleppo and the land of Niya, the elephant preserve, were joined, not for the first time, to Mukishe, and to these Pharaoh seems to have added Nuḫaṣṣi, the great steppe area south of Aleppo and east of the Orontes. The whole formed a really large and important kingdom but one not easily held together; as long as Egypt was ready to back its vassal he could command the obedience of the kinglets ruling his various provinces, but without that support he would be hard put to it to maintain his authority.

The death of Thothmes III in *circa* 1447 B.C. was almost inevitably the signal for a revolt in Syria, prompted by Mitanni. But whoever was the king of Alalakh at the time was too conscious of his need of Egyptian help to risk entangling himself with such doubtful allies as Mitanni, and so when Amenhotep II, having routed the enemy south of the Orontes, advanced to Niya the town opened its gates to him and the townspeople cheered him from the walls. It was during his reign that Niqmepa came to the throne. He was undoubtedly a member of the royal house but he does not claim for his father Idri-mi the title of king, so that he may have been a nephew of the ruler who had remained faithful to Pharaoh; and he in his turn continued to acknowledge a formal allegiance to Egypt to the extent that Egyptian symbols appear on the royal seal (Pl. 14 a). But it can have been little more than a form. The temple which he built for the city's god was not indeed of the Mitanni type, but equally it was not Egyptian, and a real vassal of Pharaoh would have been obliged to propitiate the gods of the Nile. The fact was that Egyptian suzerainty in North Syria had become a very shadowy thing while the power of Mitanni was steadily on the increase – so much so that in about 1420 B.C. Thothmes IV asked for the daughter of Artatama, the Mitanni king, in marriage and concluded a formal alliance with him. Niqmepa certainly had to walk delicately. Since his titles make no mention of Aleppo we may deduce that the sub-kingdom had become independent; indeed, he may have succeeded to no more than the old kingdom of Mukishe, and it is in that capacity, as 'king of the city-state Alalakh' that he signed a treaty with Ir-Mermer 'king of the city-state Tunip', recorded on a tablet which we found in the palace ruins; Tunip lay immediately to the south of Mukishe, and Niqmepa was apparently trying to strengthen his position. One tablet, describing the elevation of a citizen of Alalakh to a social rank which enjoyed a Hurrite name, mentions the Mitanni gods in a form which might imply direct submission to Mitanni; on the other hand another tablet, a résumé of a law-suit, describes how one Irib-khazi, a subject of Niqmepa, brought an action against Niqmepa before Shaushshatar king of Mitanni claiming to be a citizen of Hanigalbat and therefore Shaushshatar's subject, but Niqmepa won the case and Irib-khazi had to return to his service; in this case the ruler of Alalakh maintains his independence and is confirmed in it. Sidney Smith states definitely that Niqmepa was a vassal of Shaushshatar. I should rather believe that he contrived to hold the balance between the Pharaoh and the Mitanni king, each of whom probably was flattered to consider himself his suzerain; but he was sufficiently successful in his diplomacy to be able to build himself a new palace which, though not planned on a very royal scale, was at least a token of sovereignty.

Niqmepa was succeeded by his son Ilim-ilimma, a more ambitious but a less politic ruler. His great achievement

was to extend the boundaries of his kingdom so as to include both Aleppo and Niya, which his father had never
governed. How he managed to do this we do not know,
but it cannot have been by conquest because he could never
have made headway against the Hurri confederacy of which
Artatama of Mitanni was now the head, and Aleppo was
itself a Hurri state. In one of the Atchana tablets there is
evidence that he was a vassal of the Hurri; it is tempting to
assume that he had taken advantage of the treaty between
Artatama and Thothmes IV for his own aggrandizement –
Egypt was relinquishing its claims on northern Syria and
Mitanni was to be the Great Power; but the faithful servant
of Pharaoh could not shift his allegiance except at a price,
and as for the profession of vassalage, '*Paris vaut la messe*'. In
any case, Ilim-ilimma could call himself 'King of Aleppo',
and to his father's house at Alalakh he could add a building
as big again in which to conduct the business of his wider
realm.

When in 1938 and 1939 we excavated the Level IV
palace we had no hesitation at all in saying that its destruction had been due to a revolt of the inhabitants. It had been
burnt thoroughly and uniformly; Ilim-ilimma's new building, separated from the old as it was by a double wall, and
the kitchen wing, which had no inside communication with
the palace proper, had suffered equally and at the same
time. There were no bodies found, which looked as if there
had been no defence. The treasures of the upper rooms had
certainly been looted, and the archives had so far as possible
been removed to safety, which the citizens might well do
seeing that all sorts of title-deeds and legal documents of
general interest would have been kept in the palace, though
the removal seems to have been an afterthought;[1] but

1. A great many were left in the archive room, possibly as the result
of hasty sorting; a few had been dropped on the way out of the building, and a whole set were found together in the forecourt, apparently a
basketful, which implies that the palace was already on fire and the
rescuers could not get back to pick them up.

there had been no disturbance of the domestic quarters nor any salvage; judging by appearances the fire had been started simultaneously in several places, and the servants had at least not been taken by surprise. So far as we know, no other building in the city was burnt at the same time; destruction was concentrated on and confined to the royal palace.

Our conclusion was fully confirmed by the text of the Idri-mi inscription. There *was* a revolt, which apparently resulted in the death of Ilim-ilimma, and when Idri-mi did recover his kingdom he had to build a palace for himself, presumably because that of his father no longer existed. Sidney Smith points out that the death of Artatama may have tempted Ilim-ilimma to try to shake off the yoke of Mitanni. Since Aleppo, where the revolt started, was traditionally a Hurri centre any action against the Mitanni was sure to be unpopular there; but even in Mukishe the North Syrian element had always been the strongest and its citizens can have had little sympathy with Egypt, so that there too the king's policy was bound to meet with opposition. Artatama's successor, Shutarna, can have had no trouble in stirring up open rebellion against his disaffected vassal.

Idri-mi seems to have been in Alalakh when the news reached him of the outbreak at Aleppo and (probably) of his father's murder and, guessing that the trouble would spread, he with the whole of the royal family fled south along the Orontes to a city called Emar, which had been part of his mother's dowry. This would seem to have been the occasion of the burning of the Alalakh palace. But at Emar he found that his brothers, each of whom, according to custom, was regent of a city-state, were now in favour of a pro-Mitanni policy and although they did not openly turn against him were clearly not to be trusted; so 'I took to me my horse and my chariot and my squire and went up thence. I traversed the waste land and entered among the warriors who are Sutu. With him, within my covered chariot, I spent the night; the next day I departed and went to the land of Canaan. In Canaan I approached the city of Ammia. In Ammia dwelt sons of the city of Aleppo, sons of the lands Mukishe and Niya and warriors of the land Ama'u; they saw me, and behold, I was the son of their lord, and verily they assembled against me. Accordingly I led all my companions away and I abode among the 'Apiru-warriors for seven years'. The prince was of course hoping to put himself under the protection of Pharaoh, hence his flight to the south country, but he dared stop nowhere where there were men from his own land; to them he was 'the son of his father' against whom they had rebelled, and though Ammia was still directly subject to Egypt Egyptian control was not strong enough to guarantee his safety. It is interesting that he should have found refuge with a Hebrew tribe settled in the extreme north of Canaan (north of what was to be the area of Asher and Zebulon) several generations before the time when Joshua invaded the country from the south.

For seven years Idri-mi remained in exile, consulting the oracles,[1] and at last the omens proved favourable. He does not explain what they were. We have to remember that his autobiography was composed many years later and under very different conditions and he had to be careful how he expressed himself; he prudently says nothing about Egypt, but evidently he learnt during his exile that Egypt was a bruised reed and that his only hope lay in submission to the Mitanni overlord. He wrote therefore to Shutarna 'the mighty king, king of the warriors of the Hurri-land' asking

1. He says, 'I made omens from the birds clear, I examined the intestines of lambs.' Sidney Smith comments that omens from birds were common among the Hittites (a letter found at Atchana probably refers to birds kept for that purpose) and it would seem that such omens were a regular part of statecraft in Syria as in Rome (the *haruspices*). On Pl. 14 d is figured a clay model of animal intestines found at Atchana (Level VI); it is divided into squares in which are marked lumps and holes, a key for the reading of omens from the blemishes on the liver's surface. King Idri-mi presumably used a model of the sort.

to be received back into favour;[1] 'our word seemed good
to the kings of the warriors of the Hurri-land' and the conditions were duly drawn up in writing and the appropriate
sacrifices were performed and 'then I became King'. He
built ships and embarked his troops and approached the
land Mukishe by sea – i.e. he landed at his own harbour at
the mouth of the Orontes, the modern al Mina at the foot
of Mt Kasios, 'in front of the mountain', as he puts it, and
'oxen and sheep came up before me in token of friendship,
and kept on coming. As one man the lands Niya, Ama'u, and
Mukishe and the city Alalakh, my capital, turned back to
me'; his brothers too were reconciled and were confirmed
by him in their governments. This general welcome of a
king who had so long been proscribed resulted of course
from the knowledge that Shutarna approved of his return;
but nothing is said of Aleppo, which had formed part of
Ilim-ilimma's kingdom; that was now lost, and its loss
must have been one of the conditions laid down by Sutarna.
Another condition must have bound Idri-mi to play a
definite part in a war between the Hurri and the Hittites of
Anatolia who at this moment, just before the accession of
Subbiluliuma, were disorganized and more or less at their
enemies' mercy. But the inland States of the Hurri confederacy were separated from Hatti-land by the Taurus
range and could only attack along the lines of the few
passes, which were likely to be stubbornly held; the king of
Alalakh was the only one able to make a flank attack because
he alone had access to the sea and a harbour and ships of
his own; moreover, holding the Bailan Pass, he could use
the coastal road that runs from Alexandretta to the Cilician
plain. On the shores of the great Gulf there were seven
Hittite harbours, small fortified towns. 'These', says Idri-

---

1. In the inscription he describes first his return home and then his
treaty with Shutarna; but in fact either the treaty came first or else all
the preliminaries had been carried out in advance and only the formalities
were held over until they could be conducted at Alalakh. The treaty
and 'the mighty oath' were in truth very one-sided.

mi, 'I plundered. The land of *Hatte* did not assemble, and they did not march against me; what I would, that I did. I carried off their portable property . . . their trade goods and their personal possessions, and divided them up among my garrison troops, the officers my brethren and the officers I maintain; together with them I myself took my share. Then I returned to the land Mukishe and entered the city Alalakh, my capital. With the portable goods and the material acquired, with the trade goods and the household goods which I had ordered to be sent south from the land *Hatte*, I had a house built. I made my throne exactly like the thrones of the kings, the officers my state servants like the state servants of the kings, my sons like their sons; and I made the officers of my court to be as their court.'

I have described above how the citadel of Alalakh was remodelled in the later part of the Level IV period, after the destruction of the palace of Niqmepa, that the rebuilding gave it very much the air of a palace, and that the old palace site seems to have been left vacant, floored over as part of the parade-ground in front of the citadel. This accords very well with the Idri-mi autobiography; his father's palace had gone, and he builds a new one; the dates therefore fit. But Idri-mi makes it clear that his new work differed from the old – it was an out-and-out imitation of the palaces of his brother kings of the Mitanni confederacy. Niqmepa had been content with building what was really but a large private house in the best residential quarter – he was *primus inter pares* rather than monarch. Ilim-ilimma had added to that, but still lived amongst his people – and when they rose against him the house was defenceless. It looks as if Idri-mi had learned his lesson, and used the loot of the Hittite towns not to rebuild the house of his forefathers but to assure his own safety; he would live, as a king should, under the protection of his troops, in a stronghold immune from any attack by rebellious subjects; he builds his palace inside the citadel.

The changing political conditions of the time are aptly illustrated by the pottery.

At Yorghan Tepe, the site of an ancient city called Nuzu,

Fig. 18. *Examples of Nuzu Pottery*

which is near Kirkuk, east of the river Tigris, there was found a peculiar type of painted pottery dated by the tablets found associated with it to the period *circa* 1450–1350 B.C., the earliest examples being connected with the reign of

Shaushshatar king of Mitanni. At Tell Brak on the upper Khabur river the same pottery is introduced suddenly, probably about the time when Shaushshatar is in power. This pottery then, of which the distinguishing feature is a decoration in opaque white paint on a black- or brown-painted ground, can be taken as a sort of hall-mark of Mitanni influence. At Atchana one fragment and possibly a second occurred late in the Level V period, i.e. just before the time of Niqmepa. Two or three sherds could be dated to the time of Ilim-ilimma, for they were in the trench dug for the foundations of his addition to the palace. In the last phase of Level IV, after the destruction of the palace, it occurs freely; it is common in Level III and most abundant in Level II (by that time it had become a local product) and is completely absent from Level I. The meaning of this is quite clear. The pottery was invented in the East shortly before the time of Niqmepa and a few examples of the novelty filtered in to Alalakh by way of trade. Niqmepa was a contemporary of Shaushshatar, and had he really been a vassal of the Mitanni king the distinctive pottery would have been as common at Alalakh in his time as it appears to have been at Brak – and Nuzu – but the fact that not a single sherd was found shows how well he maintained his independence. Ilim-ilimma's early concessions to the Mitanni power explain the casual occurrence of fragments of the ware early in his reign, but it is significant that at the time of his death of all the thousands of clay vessels in the royal palace only thirteen were of the Nuzu type, whereas the ivory unguent-pots were in the Egyptian style; but that the ware should be common in the post-palace phase of Level IV is a testimony to Idri-mi's submission to the Mitanni overlords.

Idri-mi had reigned for thirty years when he caused the inscription to be engraved on his statue, and the occasion of his so doing was his handing over of power to his son, Adad-nirari. The reign that had begun so badly had on the whole been at least superficially successful; there had been no wars after that one profitable raid on the Hittite harbour towns, for with peace established between Egypt and Mitanni the vassals of Shutarna had no foes to meet. The main activity on which the king of Alalakh could base his claim to greatness was that he had settled on the land the Sutu, the nomad Bedouin, who had been the unstable element in his kingdom; it may have been an act of gratitude, for some of the tribe had befriended him in the days of his exile, or it may have been political foresight, for people with a stake in the country were more likely to be useful subjects than were tent-dwellers who could pack up their goods and melt away at the first signs of trouble. 'So', he says, 'I established my land'. He had built fortresses of the ancestral type and he had been punctilious in all religious observances; now he either abdicated in favour of Adad-nirari or associated the young man with himself as joint ruler (the language which he uses is ambiguous); 'in my turn I handed on the trust to the management of my son'.

The old king was well advised. It was about the year 1385 B.C. and heavy clouds were gathering on a horizon which for thirty years had been clear. The Hittites in Anatolia, old enemies of the Hurri, had been for a generation under an eclipse. They had been defeated by Mitanni and even Alalakh had been able to loot their cities with impunity; so ill had things gone with them that their king, Tudkhalia III, was at last assassinated by his own son and the throne was left free to a really capable and energetic monarch. When Idri-mi retired Subbiluliuma had been in power for only two years or so, but already he had consolidated his position and was preparing to take the offensive against North Syria, a campaign to be waged as much by diplomacy as by force of arms, though where force was needed he was ready to use it to the full. His opportunity came with a quarrel between the Hurri states and the Mitanni who for so long had controlled the confederacy; the Hittite allied himself with Artatama the Hurri king and could therefore legitimately make war on Artashumara of

Mitanni, and the Hittite army marched southwards through
the passes of the Taurus. The Mitanni forces were defeated,
but that was only the beginning. To the kings of the
Syrian city-states it was obvious enough that Subbiluliuma
envisaged the conquest of the whole country and that their
own turn would come very soon; no patched-up alliance of
the states could make headway against the invader and
piecemeal they would fall an easy prey; in their despair they
bethought themselves of their old suzerain and appealed to
Pharaoh. In the diplomatic correspondence found at Tell el
Amarna in Egypt, the archives of Pharaoh's Foreign Office,
the situation is made manifest. The king of Qatna (in
central Syria) writes to Amenhetep III: 'O my lord, even
as I bear love unto the king my lord, so also do the king of
Nuḫašši, the king of Ni-i (Niya), the king of Zinzar and the
king of Tunanat. Verily all these kings belong to the party
of my lord, are vassals of thine'. Qatna, not far from Kadesh,
really was in the Egyptian zone, but Nuḫašši and Niya had
long ceased to bear allegiance to the Pharaoh; the king of
Qatna is therefore tactfully acting as intermediary for the
northern kingdoms[1] which were more immediately threatened. But Amenhetep III was an old man who towards the
close of a peaceful reign was wholly immersed in the display
of his magnificence, in the building of temples and the
celebration of court functions; there was no question of his
undertaking a foreign campaign. He might send a few
troops into Syria when the appeals of his vassals there
grew more and more urgent, but they were only enough to
stave off internal disorders, quite insufficient to stop the
advance of the Hittites. Then Amenhetep died (1375 B.C.)
and was succeeded by the impractical visionary Akhenaten
who cared little for Egypt and not at all for Syria; Subbiluliuma with cynical correctness wrote to congratulate
him on his accession and made ready to despoil him of his
empire. It was about this time that Adad-nirari, whom we

1. The location of Zinzar and Tunanar is not known, but they were
certainly northern states.

can identify as the son of Idri-mi, wrote himself to Pharaoh (whether Amenhetep III or Akhenaten is not clear) protesting his devotion and begging for help. He reminds Pharaoh how Thothmes III had enlarged the kingdom of his own ancestor Taku and guaranteed his kingship; now the Hittites are threatening all those who were of the party of the king of Egypt. A suzerain who expects loyalty from his subjects must himself be loyal to them; 'Verily, if my lord will not agree to going out, then let my lord send as messenger one member of his council with his soldiers and with his chariotry'. The cry fell upon deaf ears; no troops were sent, and the Hittites were given a free hand. Adad-nirari died, presumably, and Takuwa succeeded him as King of Mukishe just as matters came to a head. In about the year 1370 B.C. Subbiluliuma advanced in force and drove Dushratta from the throne of Mitanni, and with the disappearance of Mitanni no organized resistance by the Syrian states was possible. 'I overpowered the land of Aleppo', boasts the Hittite king, 'and the land of Mukishe. Takuwa, the king of the city of Niya, came back to the land of Mukishe to my presence, saying "Peace".' Takuwa had probably moved the whole of his forces into the most eastern province of his kingdom to join the muster of the vassal States summoned by Dushratta of Mitanni to resist the Hittites, who had crossed to the east side of the Euphrates, but he had taken no part in the fighting. Hearing that Subbiluliuma had crushed Dushratta and then, turning west again, had captured Aleppo and was now actually encamped in Mukishe, Takuwa left his army behind and hurried home to make terms with the conqueror; his cry of 'Peace' meant unconditional surrender. But his country was not prepared to submit so tamely. 'In the rear of Takuwa' says Subbiluliuma, 'his brother Akit-Teshup again made the land Niya and the city Niya hostile and re-united six of the chief nobles. They re-united with Akia king of Arakhtu' (a town on the Euphrates) 'together with their chariotry and their soldiery. They refortified the city

Arakhtu and again became hostile. They said "Let us do battle with the great king, the king of the land Hatti". The great king, the king of the land Hatti, overpowered them at Arakhtu. Akia, king of the land Arakhtu, Akit-Teshup the brother of Takuwa and those chief nobles, all of them, he took prisoner, he ordered them to be taken to the land Hatti'.

That was the end of our Level IV.

CHAPTER VIII

Alalakh under the Hittites

Levels III and II

*

WHEN, in 1938, we excavated the palace of Niqmepa we found our task much complicated by the character of the ruins that overlay it. Close-set walls, or rather wall-foundations, ran across the whole of the western area of the palace; they were from eight to sixteen feet thick, their lower foundations were of stone – boulders, heavy limestone rubble, and slabs of basalt from the ruins of older buildings – and above that a solid mass of mud-brickwork black in colour but flecked with scraps of white lime, crumbly and difficult to distinguish from mere soil, the whole, brick and stone together, measuring as much as twelve feet in height. The builders had cut their foundation-trenches down to and sometimes below the floors of the Level IV palace, starting at the level of Idri-mi's old parade-ground which lay only four or five feet above those floors, but as soon as the new walls rose the spaces between them – the rooms, as they appear upon the plan – were filled in solidly with brick to a depth of another five feet at least. The real floors of the rooms had been weathered away and what we laid bare at first was an apparently homogeneous mass of brickwork, a huge platform with no constructional detail at all. Only as the bricks dried with exposure to the air could we with difficulty distinguish the filling from the walls, and when we removed the former there were no doorways between the 'rooms', so that the 'walls' were more accurately described as wall-foundations although they rose above ground

level. The building in fact had been raised, by the filling-in
of its lower part, on a solid base.

The SE. wall, fronting on the city, was provided with
great square buttresses set at regular intervals, and this
feature, together with the enormous strength of the whole
structure, showed it to be a fortress, and although the

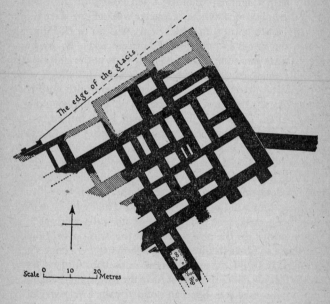

Fig. 19. *Plan of the Fortress of Level III*

evidence was rather intangible I felt justified in asserting that
it had been erected in the Level III period and continued
in use throughout the period of Level II.

Wherever, in later seasons, we dug to the west of the
Niqmepa palace we encountered more walls of the same
system; the fortress covered the whole of the NW. end of
the city. Actually we never found its limits, except for a
short stretch of walling on the NE., but the part of the

building which we did excavate measured no less than 260 by 260 feet (Fig. 19); it was by very much the largest building discovered at Atchana. A ground-plan without any doorways is a disappointing thing in that it gives no hint as to the communications between the rooms and therefore as to their use; one could distinguish a staircase and, with tolerable certainty, open courts or light-wells; but the only rooms whose character was definite were three, in the south corner, in which there was no brick filling to raise the floors but they were entirely taken up by huge terra-cotta jars sunk almost to their rims in the ground (Pl. 15 b); these rooms were really cellars in which were stored the provisions of the garrison, and although they were in use throughout the Level II period the lay-out was original and even the store-jars (which, being buried, would last indefinitely) probably belonged to Level III. Over the whole area the evidence confirmed our original view that the building was a fort and that it dated from the Level III period; it was indeed one of the two main public buildings which determined the character of the Level.

The other building was the temple. The Level IV temple had been razed and the stumps of its walls were used as foundations for the new work; but this was on very different lines so far as its internal arrangements were concerned, though it stood on precisely the same spot and its outer walls followed identical lines. As in the fort, so in the temple, the lower part was filled in solidly with brickwork to a height of six and a half feet; it could therefore be entered only by an external staircase. The interior was divided by a cross-wall into two unequal parts, at the back (i.e. on the NW. side) a wide and shallow chamber, in the front part solid brickwork at the south corner and then a very narrow passage. All the walls were very thick, implying that the building had been of considerable height. To the front of the building (i.e. against the SE. wall) had been added a portico with a very wide central entrance divided by two brick piers, a triple doorway; in front of the middle doorway there was a brick altar standing in a courtyard floored with fine white cement.

This cement floor helped us greatly in the restoration of the building, for it continued under the portico right up to the front wall of the temple proper and into the recess at the NE. end of the portico but not into the SW. recess; it

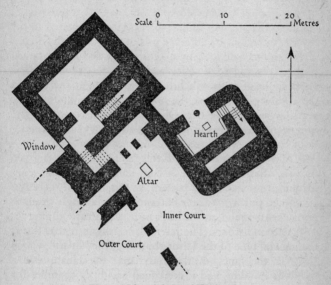

Fig. 20. *Plan of the Level III Temple*

stopped abruptly on the line of the face of the SW. jamb of the triple doorway, and in its stead we found only packed rubble. This therefore was the position of the stairs leading up to the temple; they filled that SW. recess and then turned to the right through a doorway in the temple wall and, given the normal gradient of an Alalakh stair, would by then have reached exactly the level of the temple floor. Inside the door there was a small lobby with, facing one, a door leading to the chamber at the back of the building;

the long and narrow 'passage' to the right of the lobby was a second staircase by which one mounted to the upper room. Undoubtedly the temple was a tower-like structure two storeys high and the real sanctuary was in the upper storey.

The forecourt in which the altar stood had on one side a portico or colonnade behind which there was apparently an outer court. Its SE. limits we never found, for it had been completely denuded, but on the NE. there was a second sanctuary not unlike the first but orientated in the reverse direction. Its entrance was in the NW. wall where a wide doorway divided by a central pier led into a paved room in the middle of which was a brick hearth; on the left was a flight of stairs which turned to the right and then to the right again, against the back wall of the building, to reach an upper chamber. Obviously in this case also the important room was in the upper storey and the ground-floor chamber served some minor ritual purpose.

A fairly close analogy with this temple building is given by one, admittedly of much later date but probably conforming to a traditional pattern, at Carchemish; there is a columned portico, a triple entrance-door, a single ground-floor chamber and, at the back of it, a staircase leading up to the second storey. The resemblance suggests that this is the general type of the Hittite building, the 'Hilani', which so took the fancy of the Assyrians; the Hilani was a religious building and it contained an upper chamber for the special use of the king, presumably the chamber where he himself offered sacrifice. I have already suggested that we may have a prototype of the Hilani in our Level XII temple (*v.* p. 58) but when we find it in Level III we can hardly fail to conclude that its reappearance is due to the Hittites who by now had made it their own.

The conclusion is strengthened by a tablet found on the temple site. It was actually found in the rubble foundations of the Level I temple, which would mean no more than that it antedated the erection of that building; but it had been burnt and discoloured by fire, and since the Level II temple was not destroyed by fire whereas the Level III temple was, the tablet can safely be attributed to Level III. The interest of the tablet lies not so much in its content as in its character, for it is of a type which is peculiarly Hittite and has never before been found outside the Hittite capital, Bogazköy, itself; its occurrence therefore at an outlying non-Hittite centre such as Alalakh is remarkable.

In Level III we find for the first time *bullae*, Hittite seals in the form of a flattened sphere with a hieroglyphic inscription on either face; these were the personal seals of individuals, Hittite officials living at Alalakh. A certain number of tablets were found, and these too point to a change in the racial origin at least of the upper stratum of society; not only do new forms of proper names appear, but the titles of the social classes have a different dialectical form; moreover in a series of dockets listing the distribution of grain the Babylonian or Assyrian month-names are now used for the first time at Alalakh and the measures are different from those employed in Level IV.

These archaeological facts can be translated in terms of political history.

Alalakh had surrendered to Subbiluliuma. He was not at all the kind of man to indulge in destruction for destruction's sake as did the Assyrian conquerors, but he must have been seriously annoyed by Akit-Teshup's attempt to renew the war and he must also have taken it as a warning that he could not reckon on the loyalty of the people of Mukishe. Whether he vented his wrath on king Takuwa, suspecting him of double-dealing, we do not know, but he is hardly likely to have left him upon the throne, and it looks as if the whole royal family came under his displeasure, for the citadel of Alalakh together with the royal palace that formed a part of it was destroyed by fire; and since neither the temple nor the private houses of the citizens suffered in this way the fire seems to have been intentional. He then built the huge fortress (which presumably housed also the governor) to dominate the city. He rebuilt the city temple, giving it a Hittite character, and for the use of its priests he had sent from Bogazköy, his capital, special tablets, as if he proposed to make Alalakh a Syrian centre of the Hittite religion. He brought in Hittite officials for the conduct of government and saw to it that government business was transacted on the technical model of his administration at home. We know that Subbiluliuma installed his son as king of Aleppo. We do not know whether Mukishe was included in that kingdom (which is likely enough) in which case it may have been directly under the king's son; but if not, there would almost certainly have been a Hittite governor responsible either to Aleppo or to Bogazköy; the Hittite government staff must have served under a Hittite chief.

Alalakh had lost its independence; but against the obvious proofs of a foreign administration being imposed upon the city we have one curious archaeological fact. Apart from the imported objects such as seals which would only be used by the alien officials and from the written documents of which they were the authors there is no sign of any change in the lives and habits of the citizens. The most marked feature of the period is that the painted Nuzu pottery which had been coming into fashion towards the end of Level IV now becomes the main 'luxury ware' of every private house. This pottery, as we have seen, was by origin Mitanni and was introduced to Alalakh in the time of the Mitanni suzerainty; it was indeed a symbol of the suzerain power. It was now being manufactured locally by the Alalakh potters, but one cannot believe that its origin was forgotten; its astonishing popularity during the Hittite period looks very much like an act of bravado, flaunting in the face of the conqueror the emblem of the real sentiments of the people. Side by side with the Nuzu pottery there was still in use the 'White Slip' ware which is so common in Cyprus; this was not a local fabric but was imported from somewhere in the north, but had nothing to do with the Hittites; its vogue was now lessening in face of the competition of the Nuzu pottery. We found a few fragments of local painted pottery which suggest that an attempt was even made to revive the ancient ceramic tradition which had been so strong a thousand years before. There is certainly nothing to suggest a revolution in the civil life of the state, and if the evidence be but scanty – as it is – that is because the period was a very short one. The temple and the fort are outstanding monuments, but there is little else that is individual, and the private houses are generally those of Level IV maintained in continuous occupation or, if they were built in the Level III period, they continued, like the fort, to be used in the succeeding age. The building remains convinced us that only a short lapse of time was represented and conclusive evidence that such was indeed the case was given by the imported pottery of Level II, some of which could be dated to the middle of the four-teenth century B.C. Level III therefore should fall between 1370 and about 1350 B.C.

This date, based on purely archaeological evidence, agrees well with what we know of the history of the time. In or about the year 1347 the great king Subbiluliuma died. The son who succeeded him died a few weeks later and another son, Mursilis II, ascended the throne. At once the newly-won provinces of the Hittite Empire revolted and it took seven years of hard fighting to bring North Syria back to its allegiance. Carchemish and Aleppo were both in-volved in the rebellion in spite of the fact that they had been governed by the sons of the Great King; and the example of Aleppo was certain to be followed by Alalakh. The dis-affection which had advertised itself by the use of Nuzu pottery now found full vent; to the rising of the people against their foreign masters we can attribute the burning of the Level III temple, the monument of the Hittite victory.

The revolt, in the end, failed. Mursilis recovered Aleppo and installed his nephew as governor, and Alalakh must have fallen at the same time. Probably it surrendered as soon as its more powerful neighbour had been captured;

there are no signs of wanton destruction in the residential quarters of the town such as there would have been had it succumbed to an enemy attack. The war of independence had been an interlude and now the former régime was restored; for the ordinary citizen it was little more than a change of government, and domestic life went on much as before. Judging from what we could learn of Level II the new government was liberal in its views and interfered as little as might be with the private concerns of its subjects.

A new temple was built on the site of that of Level III, but it had nothing Hittite about it; it was a one-storey building much more like those which had stood here in the old days of independence. The Hittite levels of sanctuary and courtyard remained virtually the same – there had been no such lapse of time as would result in a rise of the ground-levels – but the former portico was now incorporated in the building; it was walled across and filled in flush with the high floor of the sanctuary and instead of the internal staircase there was now a flight of steps in the thickness of the new front wall with a wide doorway giving on to a passage-like entrance-hall.[1] Facing the steps there was a doorway with a central column (this had disappeared, but the mark of it could be seen on the stone slabs of the threshold) which led into the antechamber overlying the staircase of the Hittite building; in the back wall of this there were two doors belonging to two rooms which together corresponded to the old sanctuary; it seems evident that a change of ritual had been introduced and the temple was now dedicated to a pair of deities instead of to a single god. In front of the temple the open-air altar was restored almost in the same spot, but the size of the forecourt was very much reduced, a new wall being built across it on the SE. What was done with the second sanctuary which in the Level III period had flanked the forecourt on the NE. we do

---

1. It is possible that this contained, on the right, a staircase leading to the flat roof of the antechamber; there are analogies for such in the ancient temples, but we found no evidence of it.

not know, for whatever was there had been completely denuded, but since there is a temple annexe here in Level I there was probably something of the same sort in Level II. Perhaps then, as later, there was kept here the statue of

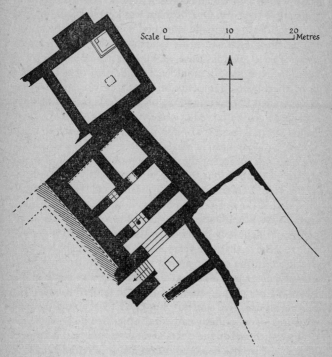

Fig. 21. *Plan of the Level II Temple*

king Idri-mi which had been spared by (or concealed from?) the Hittite conquerors and under the milder régime of Level II could safely be reinstated by the pious citizens. Certainly there was an annexe to the NW. of the temple; it was built rather later and abutted somewhat clumsily on the corner of the temple building, the brickwork of which

was actually cut back to make room for it; not enough of it
survived to give us a proper idea of its character but it was
plainly a cult building and in its north corner we found the
remains of a cupboard (only the chamfered skirting of its
walls was left) in which had been kept objects belonging to
the temple treasury. One of them was a lapis-lazuli figurine
of a goddess, originally enriched with gold, which was
purely Mesopotamian in its type and in its workmanship;
there was a splendid vase of blue paste, imitation lapis-
lazuli, with a handle moulded in the form of a couchant
lion; there were fragments of vessels of variegated glass,
the so-called Phoenician glass, of quite exceptional quality,
a human figurine carved in bone, bone inlay – the head and
wings and tail from a wooden unguent-box in the form of
a duck, a human head in glazed frit, etc. My first and natural
impulse was to accept these various objects as illustrating
the art of the day, but they do not necessarily do anything
of the sort. A fragment of a blue paste bowl with its handle
moulded in the form of a couchant lion, a companion piece
to the vase just mentioned, was found by us in Level VI
and could definitely be dated to that period, and it is difficult to believe that 400 years later a craftsman should have
produced in the same material a vase so similar in style; it
is much more probable that the vase also was made in the
Level VI period and preserved in the temple treasury for
four centuries. We are not surprised to see amongst the
treasures of a modern cathedral objects which piety has
preserved there for 500 years and more, and in this respect
human nature has changed not at all. In a temple at Ur at
the end of the Late Babylonian period the statue of the
goddess had a necklace some of the beads in which were of
the Sargonid time, fifteen centuries before; that was perhaps
an extreme case, but the practice is so general that where an
object is found in a temple its date should be *ipso facto* considered suspect. The contents of such a treasury do not then
necessarily illustrate the art and craft of the time to which
the temple belongs, but the more diverse they are in date

the more interesting they are as proving the continuity of the cult tradition and the religious care with which *ex votos* might be safeguarded.

This conservatism has preserved for us some of the architectural decoration of the Level II temple. Invariably the ruins that we find are disappointing in the picture that they give of the original building. We unearth only the foundations or, at most, the stumps of walls, and where the building material is mud-brick these have necessarily a very beggarly appearance. What we have to remember is that the mud-brick walls are the constructional core; whatever decoration the original building possessed was applied decoration. The actual surface of the walls would have been concealed by frescoes (for which we had evidence in the palace of Yarim-Lim) or by panels of cedarwood; these have naturally perished. But there were other forms of decoration which, in so far as they were removable, would either be carried off if city and temple were captured by an enemy or piously taken over for a new building if such were designed to replace the old. The Level I temple in its latest phase was adorned with basalt sculptures of lions all of which were broken and imperfect, damaged figures re-used in spite of the damage; as a fragment of one of them was discovered in the foundations of the earliest phase of the Level I temple it is obvious that the lions belong to Level II at least, and may even be earlier (in which case they would still have been used in the Level II temple). The lions are all corner-stones; they stood at the angles of the masonry, the body of the animal carved in low relief on the face of the side wall while from the front wall projected the head and forefeet, carved in the round (Pl. 18). Probably our lions formed the corner-stones of the jambs of the temple doorways – their usual position was at a doorway, guarding the entrance – and probably too the temple façade was adorned with stone reliefs such as the Ṭudkhalia slab which I shall describe later, when dealing with the Level I temple; even with this much of restoration the bare ruins of our discovery are transfigured and assume a certain splendour. But the lions have further importance as monuments for the history of art. In the 'Syro-Hittite' period gateway lions of this sort are so regular a convention as to be almost the hall-mark of North Syrian art; the majority of them can be dated between the tenth and the seventh centuries B.C., only one, a much battered specimen from the south gate of Carchemish, being very much earlier.[1] Now for the first time we have a series of lion sculptures which cannot be later than the fourteenth century B.C., and it is interesting to observe how widely they differ in style one from another. No fixed convention has been arrived at, but the artists are still experimenting; though their function is identical the animals are individuals, not examples of a type. The Atchana lions are early forerunners of the whole series of Syro-Hittite lions; quite possibly we can go further and say that the huge lions and human-headed bulls which guarded the palaces of Assyrian kings were derived ultimately from a Syrian school of art whose beginnings we can see in the temple sculptures of Level II at Alalakh.

As has been explained above, the great fortress built by the Hittites in the Level III period was re-used in Level II. This was to be expected. The massive walls of Subbiluliuma's building would not have suffered at all in the short space of time which we must attribute to Level III, and the next generation was sure to utilize them. We did find evidence of minor internal rearrangements carried out in the period of Level II, which again is no more than one would expect in the course of a century, but, apart from the cellars with their great store-jars, there was nothing to tell us of the use of the particular rooms or to give any detailed historical information; we only know that the fortress, together probably with the official residence of the governor or king inside it, continued in use.

The city wall, on the other hand, was entirely rebuilt. When we were excavating, in 1937, the private houses of

1. This is my opinion; not all authorities are agreed on the point.

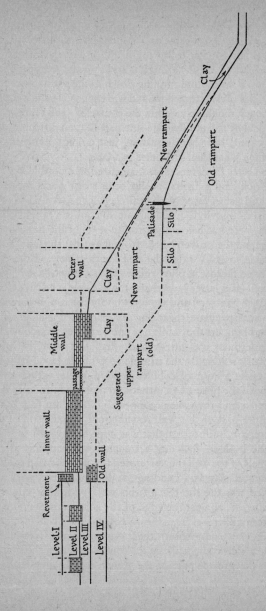

Fig. 22. *Section through the Town Wall*

Level I
Level II
Level III
Level IV

Revetment

Inner wall

passage

Middle wall

Old wall

Clay

Outer wall

New rampart

Suggested upper rampart (old)

Clay

Silo

Silo

Palisade

New rampart

Old rampart

Clay

the upper levels, we came on the inner face of the town wall of Level II and after following it up for a distance of some 150 feet cut a section through it and into the steep slope of the edge of the mound running down to the plain. Since this had always been a steep slope and was exposed to the weather it had been much denuded in the course of 3000 years and a great deal of the old defence-line had slipped downhill and disappeared, but there remained just enough evidence to determine what their character had been.

The Level III defences had consisted in a double wall of mud-brick rising from the lip of a steep glacis made of earth and ashes faced with stiff clay. The Level II people destroyed this wall (only about five of its foundation-courses were left below the ground-level of the new town) and heaped the broken bricks from it against the face of the old glacis so as to widen the base for their new work; they must have faced the piled rubble with a revetment of clay or brick – the latter is perhaps more likely – but that had long since vanished and we found only the rough core and could but speculate regarding its original finish. On this widened rampart they built not one but three parallel walls. The innermost was fifteen and a half feet wide, its mud-brickwork resting on the trimmed top of the Level III wall. Then came a floor of cobbles bedded in clay which must have been the floor of an intramural passage four and a half feet wide, and then the second wall, about ten feet thick. The inner part of this wall rested simply on the soil of the old rampart, but because that was none too good a foundation the builders had dug a trench corresponding to the outer half of the wall they proposed to build and had packed it with stiff clay as a bedding for the mud-brickwork. So denuded was the site that of this wall we found only two bricks *in situ*, against the edge of the cobbled passage. At a distance of four feet from the outer face of the wall (as given by the clay foundation) there was a second clay-filled trench which could only be the foundation of a third wall, but as the greater part of the trench had been weathered away to the existing slope of the mound's face we had no means of judging of the wall's width. But in spite of that we can say that in Level II the town defences were more elaborate than they had ever been before; the rampart with its sloped glacis was a traditional feature, but the triple wall, with its total width of more than forty feet, was without precedent.

The relation of the wall to the private houses made it certain that this enormous work of fortification dated to fairly early in the Level II period if not actually to its beginning. It is not easy to explain why it was undertaken. The Level III wall had presumably been built by Subbiluliuma at the same time as the great fortress, and if the revolt against the Hittites which marked the transition to Level II ended as I think the evidence shows it did in the surrender of the city, not in its capture by assault, Subbiluliuma's wall must have been intact and might well have served all the needs of the city. Possibly the governor installed by Mursilis, having no confidence in North Syrian loyalty, decided to turn Alalakh into a stronghold which he could maintain against a fresh general rebellion. If that were the case he was well advised, for the spirit of revolt was by no means dead; but we have no knowledge of any political happenings at this time which would have made the task of refortifying the city immediately urgent.

The period indeed seems to have been as quiet as it was prosperous. The private houses that we excavated (admittedly they were in the best residential quarter) were large and well-built, more or less of the 'courtyard' type with the rooms opening on to a central light-well, and the thickness of walls and the presence of staircases showed that part of the building at any rate had been two storeys high. One was remarkable in having its front door flanked by big half-columns in mud-brick. Lavatories with cemented floors and kitchens with hearths and ovens could generally be recognized, but the use of other rooms could seldom be guessed; the much-ruined walls did not rise, as a rule, much more than a foot above the floor and very often could be traced only by their foundations. One social change was obvious; the habit of burying the dead on the household premises was becoming more common; the

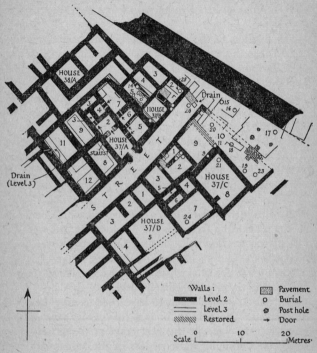

Fig. 23. *Plans of private houses of Level II*

graves were sometimes under the floors of the rooms (there seemed to be no rule as to which room should be chosen for the purpose) and sometimes in an open court at the back of the house. Such courts were not indeed universal, but they were by no means rare; often their main use appeared to be for the digging of rubbish-pits, which were as numerous in this as in any period. I have several times had occasion to speak of 'rubbish-pits', and that is the most convenient term, but it is not necessarily the true description. Often these pits, which might be fifteen or twenty feet deep, were intended simply as receptacles for refuse, as was, for instance, the case with the pits attached to the Level V temple in which we found the discarded *ex votos* from the shrine; but sometimes they were really sewage-pits, and though they might contain a certain amount of broken pottery that was an accidental intrusion. Sewage-pits were more often attached to houses standing in the middle of the town whereas buildings near the city wall could pipe their drainage out through the rampart; but the presence of two or three pits (of either sort) in the back court of a house did not constitute any objection to putting a burial there; indeed, the disposal of the dead seems to have been curiously unceremonious. The graves and the rubbish-pits with their contents of pottery, etc., were the more valuable because it was seldom that a complete vessel could be found in houses so badly denuded as were those of Level II; they supplied the intact examples while the houses yielded an immense amount of broken sherds and reliable evidence for their date.

The 'White Slip Ware' which was so common in Level IV had now gone quite out of fashion – indeed, there was not one fragment of it which we could unhesitatingly attribute to Level II, though one or two possibly belonged. It had been ousted by the Nuzu painted ware, but the use of this is perhaps no longer necessarily to be regarded as a challenge to the authority of a foreign government; it was now the standard 'luxury' product of the local potters and its political implications were probably of secondary interest, so much so that its most characteristic form owed nothing at all to Hurri or Mitanni prototypes. I have described how this really attractive painted pottery originated in the East and encouraged apparently by the Mitanni kings was exported to or reproduced by all the countries under

Mitanni influence, from Nuzu east of the Tigris to Alalakh close to the Mediterranean coast. Over the whole of that wide area vases of the same shapes painted with identical designs came into general use; so uniform is the style that it would, I think, be impossible to decide on internal evidence whether any particular example of it was found, or made, at Nuzi, on the Khabur river or on the lower Orontes. But at Alalakh in Level II we find a whole range of vessels of the same shapes and the same fabric as the normal Nuzu pots but with a design which is not Eastern at all but palpably borrowed from the art of Crete (Pl. 16 a). It is always the same design basically, with very slight modifications, and it is remarkably like what we see on vases of the 'Palace' style from Knossos, but the difficulty is that those are older than the Alalakh vases by about a hundred and fifty years. Had the Alalakh potter employed a number of different Cretan patterns the problem of how the time gap was bridged would have been almost insoluble, since neither country has produced any intermediate link – indeed we know that in Crete the fashion had died out completely after 1400 B.C.; but the general similarity of all the Alalakh pieces does suggest that all are derived from a single original. I cannot but think that a fine Cretan vase had been preserved at Alalakh, probably in the temple treasury, possibly in a private collection, and in the Level II period a working potter saw and was struck by the unusual design and copied it on his own pots, believing that the current craze for Aegean art would ensure a ready sale. In this he was right and the single model available had to be reproduced *en masse*; it was clear that no self-respecting gentleman of Alalakh could afford to be without one, and in the richer houses we even found sets of what, since the style is peculiar to the Amq, we named 'Atchana ware'.

That Aegean art was popular is proved by the fact that Mycenaean vases were now beginning to be imported (Pl. 16 (b). At Alalakh there was no colony of Mycenaean merchants such as at this time existed at Ugarit, further to the south, but Ugarit was a harbour town whereas Alalakh lies well inland; it is likely enough that there was a colony of the sort at al Mina, the port of Alalakh through which imports from the Aegean would come, but the agents of the Greek firms would have no business in the interior because when once goods had been landed from aboard ship their land transport would naturally be the affair of Asiatic carriers. Alalakh was in no sense an emporium of Aegean trade, but it appreciated and took its share of what that trade brought in, just as it forwarded to al Mina, for export to the Greek world, merchandise from Mesopotamia and from as far afield as Lake Van in the shadow of the Caucasus. Mycenaean vases were still a luxury; the best that we found was one of the big two-handled craters painted with a chariot design which seem to have been the peculiar product of Cyprus; it had been kept in the temple treasury. Of course the Mycenaean trade does not by itself explain the 'Atchana style', for that is derived from the older Cretan art which the Mycenaeans had destroyed, but the trade is only a revival of an oversea commerce which had been interrupted by the Mycenaean conquest of Knossos. I have already pointed out the close connexion between the architecture and the fresco-painting of Alalakh in the Level VII period and that of Crete; a chance discovery in Level II makes the connexion even more obvious.

Alongside one of the Level II houses (House 39/C) which contained a great deal of pottery, including much 'Atchana' ware, there was a rubbish-pit contemporary with the building, as was proved by our finding in it a fragment of an 'Atchana' vase which actually fitted on to a fragment found inside the house; at the bottom of the pit there was a stone lamp in the Cretan 'Palace' style. It is the capital, or basin, of a columnar lamp carved in fine red marble (Pl. 17 b); the basin is divided into twelve small compartments, communicating with each other and with the larger central compartment, to take twelve wicks; the sides of the compartments, as well as the design in relief on the outside of the lamp, show the lobed design characteristic of Crete, and the shape of the lamp as a whole, and in particular the two curious pendants, are exactly paralleled at Knossos, where too the lamps are of the same material. My first and natural assumption when the lamp was found was that here we had a direct import from Crete. As against this there is the fact that the red marble of which our lamp, like several from Knossos, is made is not found in Crete at all but is found in Asia Minor (it is called 'Lydian marble'); moreover, the carving of our lamp is not quite finished and it seems unlikely, considering that it is the finest known of its class, that a Cretan sculptor would not have troubled to finish it before sending it abroad for sale. It is possible that the lamps which we call Cretan were in some cases really imports from Asia and that the style originated on the mainland. In any case we have here a work typical of Cretan art which, by all analogy, must date from before 1400 B.C. but was preserved at Alalakh until, badly damaged, it was thrown away some time between 1350 and 1275 B.C. and probably nearer to the end of that period than to its beginning; it is therefore not fantastic to suggest that a painted clay vase may have survived equally long and served as a model for the potter of Alalakh.

If I have harped at length on the subject of the 'Atchana' ware it is not without reason. When the first pieces of it were found the Cretan origin of the ornament was at once recognized by everyone, including Sir Arthur Evans, who published them in the *Journal of Hellenic Studies* (1935), and since the date of Level II was not yet known the chronological difficulty did not arise and it was assumed that the Atchana copies were more or less contemporary with the Knossos originals. When the date of Level II was fixed, involving a wide time-gap, we were faced with one of those problems which from time to time confront the archaeologist when facts apparently inconsistent have to be reconciled; the solution must always depend upon a theory, which may not be generally accepted, but which although not provable does not offend probability too much. The 'Atchana' pottery seemed to afford a good illustration of archaeological method in such cases.

Common as were the Nuzu and Atchana wares in the better-class houses the distribution of the sherds was curious; in House 37/A there were numerous sherds in the entrance-room and hardly a single piece elsewhere; House 37/C had a few good sherds in room 2 and a great number in the entrance-chamber, room 1, all in the central part of the room in front of the street door; the bulk of the pieces found in the whole area lay in the street in front of and between the doors of the houses A and C. In this part of the street particularly and in rooms 1 and 2 of House 37/C we found quantities of bronze arrow-heads and a few clay sling-bolts; a narrow cupboard-like room (5) in House 37/C was full of clay sling-bolts and *ballista*-balls, a regular armoury; the walls of the houses showed signs of burning. It is clear that there had been fighting in this quarter of the town and that the houses had been pillaged and set on fire, and it can hardly be accidental that the Nuzu and 'Atchana' pottery had been collected and smashed, mostly in the street, at the time of the looting. It is further to be noted that the Level II temple was not destroyed by fire, and that in Level I no Nuzu or 'Atchana' pottery ever occurs. In my preliminary report on the season's work I suggested that there was here evidence of an internal revolt against an unpopular and probably governing section of the inhabitants, a rich class which favoured this luxury ware which with their elimination passed out of vogue; but it should be possible to connect the event with something in political history now that we have, what we had not when my report was written, an approximate *terminus ante quem* for the end of Level II; as I shall show later, Level I cannot have begun later than about 1270 B.C.

After a long period of peace during which the Hittites had consolidated their position in Syria Ramses II of Egypt attempted to revive the colonial empire of the XVIIIth

Dynasty pharaohs. In his fourth year he pushed forward as far as the Dog River north of Beyrouth where his monument can still be seen cut in the rock, and in the following year (c. 1289 B.C.) fought the great but indecisive battle of Kadesh. In that battle the king of Aleppo fought on the side of the Hittites[1] and presumably the minor state of Mukishe was equally involved. But four or five years later when Ramses, having secured northern Palestine, advanced into Syria proper, Aleppo revolted against the Hittites and made common cause with Egypt. We know that in this Aleppo did not stand alone, and although Mukishe is not specifically mentioned (the cuneiform text is incomplete) it almost certainly joined the rebels. Muwatallis, the Hittite Great King, crushed the movement and Aleppo and its associates had to sign a treaty of submission, this shortly before the year 1280 B.C. when Muwatallis died. In 1273 B.C. the new Hittite Great King Hattusilis made with Ramses 'the good treaty of peace and of brotherhood, setting peace between them forever'; the Egyptian version of the treaty says nothing as to the boundaries between the two kingdoms, but the Bogazköy text shows that the Hittite king continued to control Amor on the Upper Orontes, so that Alalakh was well within the Hittite zone.

At some time then after the battle of Kadesh Mukishe changed sides in the war between the Hittites and the Egyptians. We have been able to see that ever since the time of the XIIth Dynasty there had been a pro-Egyptian party at Alalakh which had been refounded or reinforced when Thothmes III established Taku on the throne of Mukishe and Nuḫaŝŝi; all the kings of the Niqmepa dynasty were ready to profess at least a nominal allegiance to Pharaoh. Although under the Hittite régime the old royal family had presumably ceased to rule, yet there is no reason

1. In the great Ramesside reliefs adorning the temple of Abu Simbel the routed Asiatics are represented as swimming across the Orontes and the King of Aleppo is held head downwards by his soldiers so that he may disgorge the water he had swallowed.

to suppose that it had been exterminated; much more likely it continued to form part of the aristocracy of the city and had a definite following; a revolt against the Hittites would naturally be headed by the great families which had been shorn of their prerogatives by the Hittite government, and the houses from which we draw our evidence are the big houses in the best residential quarter of the town, just those which would belong to the local aristocracy. The facts obtained by excavation seem to me to be most consistent with the view that the old nobility of Alalakh in conjunction with the nationalist party of Aleppo (where the Hittite government must have been weakened by the defeat of its forces at Kadesh) opened negotiations with Egypt and engineered a revolt which was by no means to the taste of the majority of the citizens. Very soon the revolt was crushed by Muwatallis and either the Hittites or the pro-Hittite party in the town revenged themselves on the leaders of the rising. In that case Level II ended between 1285 and 1283 B.C.

CHAPTER IX

The End of Alalakh

Level I

*

WHEN we began to dig at Atchana the first impression we got was that Level I was a poor period and short-lived, representing the final decadence of the city. Gradually however we were forced to revise this view. Some of the house sites showed two distinct strata of buildings while other houses had undergone repairs and alterations implying a considerable lapse of time. Then it was found that the temple had been rebuilt at the beginning of the period, rebuilt again on different lines and at last allowed to sink into decay in what really was a decadent phase. Since the evidence seemed quite clear that Alalakh had been finally destroyed in 1194 B.C. a date early in the fourteenth century was indicated for the start of the period. This was confirmed by the imported pottery. Throughout the period Mycenaean vases (Pl. 16 b) were in general use – they are found in buildings of all classes and in quite poor graves – and in view of what is known as to their date it would be impossible to attribute them all to the last part of the thirteenth century. As it is, we are bound to modify by the evidence of Atchana the belief of many classical archaeologists that the manufacture of these vases ceased in about 1235 B.C.; it is certain that they continued freely in use at Alalakh until the fall of the city in 1194 and since they were imported, not locally made, the manufacture of them must have gone on until practically that time. But some of the types are definitely early and their occurrence in Level I demands for the period a *terminus post quem* not long after the turn of the fourteenth century.

The sudden and complete disappearance of the painted Nuzu and 'Atchana' pottery, now supplanted by the Mycenaean, must have a social and political significance. Not less remarkable is the very great increase in the proportion of cremation burials. During the greater part of the history of Alalakh ordinary inhumation burial had been the absolute rule. A single cremation burial was doubtfully attributed to Level IV (it might have belonged to Level III), two to Level II or possibly III; in the case of those levels there was always, of course, the risk of graves being destroyed by later diggers of graves or of foundation trenches, but a fair proportion would survive. In the case of Level I on the other hand while the graves of the earlier phase were subject to the same risk during the lifetime of the town the vast majority of them all have disappeared owing to the denudation of the mound's surface during the last 3000 years. Cremation graves were shallow, set but little below the floor of a house, and the rain, the wind, and the plough have swept away all the buildings of the later phase and most of the foundations of the earlier. We recorded five more or less intact cremation burials belonging to Level I, but traces of such burials from which all the furniture had gone were met with constantly; inhumation graves would be dug more deeply, but we recorded only three as being preserved with their contents. In Level I therefore the practice of cremation, which had before been a rare exception, becomes at least as common as burial. This change too is socially significant.

It is generally agreed that cremation was introduced into Syria from Asia Minor, and it is only after the great invasion of Syria in 1194 B.C. that the custom becomes really common; thus, for example, at Carchemish it is unknown before that date and after it, in the 'Syro-Hittite' period, becomes the absolute rule. At Atchana it appears earlier, at first in a few isolated cases but in the thirteenth century on a large scale. This must be interpreted to mean that in the fourteenth century a small number of individuals from a country practising cremation moved into the kingdom of Mukishe and in time were buried there according to their ancestral rites, but that the thirteenth century saw such immigration *en masse* and the northerners (as we must

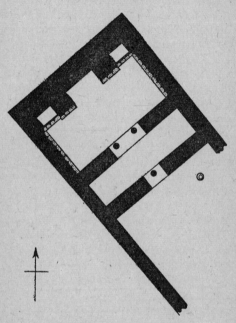

Fig. 24. *Plan of Level I (A) Temple*

suppose them to have been) came to form a very considerable part of the whole population. That much we can learn from the graves, but for further information we must examine other evidence.

The temple of Level II was dismantled and on the top of the stumps of the old walls new stone foundations were laid – heavy rubble blocks weighing on the average half a ton each – then polished basalt slabs and above these the walls carried up in mud-brick and timber. The size of the building was therefore the same, but its ground-plan was different from the old. It consisted of two rooms only. From the forecourt, in which was a finely-constructed brick-lined well, a doorway which, judging from its width of eight feet probably had a central column, led into a shallow antechamber; facing the entrance was the doorway into the sanctuary, an opening fourteen and a half feet wide divided by two columns.[1] In the back wall of the sanctuary were three recesses of which the middle one, in line with the two doorways of sanctuary and antechamber, was open, lined with wooden panelling, but the other two were masked by basalt slabs with a screen above set back slightly from the line of the intervening buttresses. I do not know any parallel for these hidden recesses which we of course found empty – in fact, the SW. recess was ruined down to ground level; but embedded in the brickwork behind the NE. recess there were a bronze dagger, a vessel of polychrome glass, an alabaster vase and some pottery which we can only reckon as part of a foundation-deposit; I imagine that the recesses contained offerings dedicated at the time of the building of the temple.

This temple had been burnt to the ground and promptly rebuilt, but with a different character. The level of the sanctuary building was raised so that the polished basalt slabs of the old walls were now buried under the floor; the recesses in the back wall disappeared and the sanctuary door was narrowed to eight feet (it may have had a central column) while the antechamber was cut up by cross walls into three, a small passage-room with a little chamber on either side of it. To bridge the difference in level between the sanctuary building and the forecourt there was built against the front wall of the former a stone platform through the centre of which ran a flight of three shallow steps

1. And probably flanked by lion sculptures; but of this we could not be sure.

flanked by the old lion sculptures salved from the Level II temple; they were no longer used for their original purpose as corner-stones (one indeed was only a fragment, head and forefeet without a body, so that it could not have been so used) but were embedded in the platform with only the

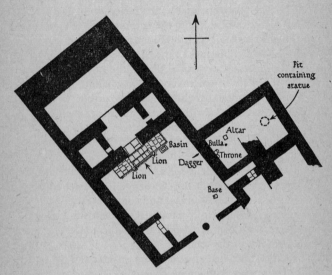

Fig. 25. *Plan of Level I (B) Temple*

heads projecting; they may have had a low coping above them, but they were now a purely decorative, not a constructional, feature. The arrangement of steps with a platform on either side is reminiscent of the façade of the Niqmepa palace and anticipates the great approach to the palace and temple of tenth-century Carchemish. When we lifted the masonry of the steps we found that one of the slabs forming the treads was a royal relief of Tudkhalia, Great King of the Hittites in 1250 B.C. (Pl. 15 a), laid face downwards and turned to base uses.

In front of the sanctuary was the forecourt, measuring about forty-five by forty-two feet, having a columned entrance at its SE. end and chambers in its south corner; on the NE. side of it there was a separate building (occupying the site of the second sanctuary of the Level III temple) which so far as we could judge from the scanty remains that survived was not of temple form but a complex of rooms opening off a passage. In one of the rooms a pit had been dug and sealed with great blocks of stone; beneath them we found the fragments of the statue of king Idri-mi (Pl. 12 a), collected and hidden for safety. In the next room was the broken throne of the Idri-mi statue, a basalt altar decorated with swans' heads (Pl. 19 a), and a seal inscribed in Hittite hieroglyphs, an ivory libation-spoon with a human hand supporting the bowl and a much-defaced limestone figure of a seated goddess. In the forecourt, not far from a basalt trough let into the floor, there was a splendid ritual spear-head of bronze, the blade gripped by two figures of lions cast in the round (Pl. 17 a); in the sanctuary itself a very remarkable carving of a human face broken off from a basalt relief. All these objects had been scattered here at the time of the temple's destruction, but they did not lie upon its original floor. During the lifetime of the temple the courtyard floor had risen, with successive resurfacing, by more than a foot, with the curious and unseemly result that not only were the bottom treads of the sanctuary steps buried but the feet of the lions also had disappeared and only their heads showed with the chins scarcely above ground level; the temple façade had become a mere travesty of its former state, something so different that we called this top level 'Phase 3', the last phase of decadence.

In the room at the south corner of the forecourt we found a 'bulla' seal engraved with a hieroglyphic inscription unfortunately illegible, but the seal found in the NE. annexe bore an inscription which could be read, 'Pa-lu-wa, son of the King, lord of the land', a replica of the text on a seal-impression also found in Level I. The bronze spear-

head with its lions is curiously like a figure of the 'Dagger
God' carved on the face of the rock at Yasilikaya close to
Bogazköy, part of a series of Hittite reliefs of the thirteenth
century B.C. The Tudkhalia relief is a Hittite royal monument which must originally have stood in the earlier temple
of Level I. If we relate these discoveries with the evidence
of foreign immigration already described the story becomes
clear.

When Hattusil, the Hittite Great King, in 1273 concluded peace with Egypt he was undoubtedly influenced by
fear of the growing power of Assyria which, under Shalmaneser I, now threatened from the East the Syrian possessions of the Hittites. To assure these a certain amount of
reorganization was necessary. In the first place the citadel
fortress was rebuilt. Constructed at the beginning of the
Level III period, 100 years before, it was probably falling
into decay and quite possibly had suffered damage in the
pro-Egyptian rising of ten years before; in any case its walls
were now razed and on the stumps of them a new building
erected. Very little remains of this, thanks to the denudation
of the Atchana mound, but the stone foundations show
that it adhered for the most part to the old plan. The fortress
would, almost certainly, be garrisoned by regular troops of
the Hittite army, but that was not assurance enough. Bitter
experience had proved that Alalakh was not a trustworthy
subject, and although the pro-Egyptian faction had been
scotched and with the treaty now in force could no longer
look to Egypt for support still the bulk of the citizens were
a North Syrian stock whose loyalty to the Anatolian Hittites
was apt to be more opportunist than heartfelt. The Great
King decided that what was wanted was a Hittite leavening
of the lump. Apparently one of his sons, Paluwa, was installed as governor to give effect to the new policy and a
stream of Anatolian immigrants was directed on Alalakh.
The new temple was presumably built under Hittite direction; the spear-head recalling the 'Dagger God' of Bogazköy
may well mean that a definitely Hittite cult was introduced

into the main sanctuary of the city, and the Tudkhalia relief certainly proves that the temple was under direct royal patronage; with all this the disappearance of the Nuzu and Atchana pottery, which we last saw being smashed up in the streets and in the houses of Egyptian sympathizers, is quite consistent. The first phase of Level I therefore represents a deliberate attempt by the Hittites to make Alalakh an outpost of Bogazköy.

Phase 2 marks the failure of that attempt. Even before Tudkhalia's death Tukulti-Inurta of Assyria, son of Shalmaneser, was invading northern Syria and very soon, by force of arms and by intrigue, he succeeded in turning the vassal states against their masters. The mere burning of the temple at Alalakh might have been regarded as an accident, but when we find that it is rebuilt on different lines recalling the national buildings of a glorious past and Tudkhalia's monument bearing the royal image is dishonoured and set to be trampled under foot, then we cannot but recognize the evidence of yet one more revolt against the Hittite suzerainty. The signal for revolt may well have been the fall of Babylon, which was captured by the Assyrians about 1241 B.C., and by that time the Hittites were too exhausted to make any real effort to recover their position; indeed their own home-land was now threatened by invasion from the west, and about the year 1200 B.C. the royal archives of Bogazköy come to a sudden end; the Hittite capital had been engulfed by the first wave of that great movement of dispossessed migrants which was to change the face of the eastern Mediterranean world.

Alalakh then succeeded in rebellion not by its own strength but by the weakness of its overlords and the moral if not the material support of Assyria; it had not the means or the energy to take advantage of that success. The rebuilding of the temple was a natural, almost an inevitable, gesture, but it seems to have been little more. The city still enjoyed a measure of prosperity. The private houses of Level I are sometimes quite large, and though the best of them were built in Phase I they were still inhabited and apparently well maintained in the later part of the period; the prevalence of Mycenaean pottery shows that there was a flourishing foreign trade, and the local industries were active – a goldsmith's workroom in the corner of a house near the city wall produced a number of heavy gold ingots, some with bits snipped off them, and small gold earrings. But the squalid neglect from which the temple suffered is enough to prove the general decline which no admixture of northern blood was able to arrest; our first impression of the decadence of the Level I period was mistaken for the period as a whole but is correct for the close of it. For this was the end. The great folk-movement of 'the Peoples of the Sea' which overwhelmed Bogazköy turned southward into Syria, the main host advancing by land, accompanied by their women and children in heavy two-wheeled ox-carts, the fleet keeping pace with it down the Syrian coast. One by one the cities fell before them and were laid waste, and the survivors of the defeated states swelled the ranks of the invaders. Carchemish was taken, and Aleppo; at Alalakh the burnt ruins of the topmost houses show that the city shared the fate of its more powerful neighbours. This was in the year 1194 B.C.[1]

The complete destruction of the city is aptly epitomized by the incident of the Idri-mi statue; the man who at the risk of his life collected the fragments of the broken figure and hid them under the temple floor never came back to recover them. About fifty years later an attempt was made to recolonize the deserted site, but by that time the brick rubble from the fallen walls had buried all the temple furniture that strewed the court and all knowledge of them had passed out of mind. Above the temple ruins foundations of heavy stones were laid for a reconstruction which

1. The fifth year of the reign of Ramses III. The story of the defeat of the Peoples of the Sea on the borders of Egypt is told in the reliefs and inscriptions of Ramses' great temple at Medinet Habu, opposite Thebes (Luxor).

perhaps was never carried to a finish; near the old citadel we found some meaningless patches of cobble foundations which seemed to belong to this late time; a single cremation-burial contained a scarab of Ramses VI and must therefore have been set in position soon after 1140 B.C., but these were the only signs of any occupation of Alalakh after the destruction of 1194. Had that occupation been on a considerable scale or had it lasted for any length of time some evidence of it would inevitably have survived; its buildings might have been denuded away, but the soil would have retained at least a few potsherds of the later age; but there was nothing of the sort. When a serious attempt at resettlement was made Alalakh was abandoned and a new town was constructed on the prehistoric mound of Ta'yinat, three-quarters of a mile away; the history of Alalakh really ends with the invasion of the Peoples of the Sea.

CHAPTER X

The Port of Alalakh; Posideïum and the Greek World

*

UNDOUBTEDLY the destruction of Alalakh involved that of its harbour town also, but whereas the city never recovered the harbour was too valuable to be left long desolate; it was rebuilt and remained in use for another 700 years. It is therefore to the harbour, al Mina, that we must turn for the continuation of our history.

When in 1935 I went to look for the right site on which to dig I was convinced that the mouth of the river Orontes must have played a very important part in the overseas commerce of a land whose exposed and rocky coast so seldom affords a safe anchorage for ships; the broad river winding through the flat alluvial plain was an ideal shelter for the small mercantile craft of the ancient world and could never have been overlooked. I was therefore astonished when my enquiries as to where there was a mound near the river's mouth were met by the assurance that there did not exist anything of the kind. A visit to the area seemed to confirm this disappointing reply; but as I came near the modern customs sheds (for the river is still a port for sailing-ships) the track ran between low broken banks and on one side the ground sloped up gently for a few feet to where there stood the whitewashed domed tomb of an Alaouite saint with its wild olive tree and a barn-like structure for the use of pilgrims, and I saw fragments of pottery sticking out from the roadside bank and more littering the slope to the tomb. The first potsherd that I picked up was from an Athenian vase of the fifth century B.C. Here then was an ancient site, but where was the mound? A walk across the ploughland answered the question, for just beyond the tomb the ground broke away in a low cliff at the foot of which one could trace a dried river-bed (Pl. 24 a). The Orontes, which runs some two or three hundred yards away to the east, had at one time filled this now dry course; I felt sure that there had been a big mound here which the river had then swept away, leaving only the low rise of its inland fringe. Here a local legend helped. About a hundred and fifty years ago, I was told, the Orontes, which then ran much as it does now, suddenly in flood-time changed its course westwards. The fields were flooded, crops were swept out to sea, and the hill on the side of which the tomb stood was eaten away by the rushing waters. Faced with the ruin of all their lands the people crowded to the mosque praying for help, but the floods only grew worse and at last the tomb of Sheikh Yusuf itself, on the very brink of the crumbling cliff, seemed to be doomed. Then the Saint arose in his wrath and rebuked the river, bidding it go back instantly to its own place, and at once the flood receded, and there was Orontes in its old bed and the fields showing again; so the people built a shelter-hut alongside the tomb and the pilgrims go there to this day.

Such was the story, based certainly upon a genuine occurrence which may well have happened more than once; it accounts for the disappearance of the harbour mound, but the sad fact remains that the mound has disappeared and with it all the history stored in the successive ruin-strata of which such a mound is made. We dug what was left, the outskirts of the town at the time when it extended farthest to the west, but all the earliest levels closer to the river bank had been swept away into the sea.

Actually ten levels remained. Each of them overlapped the one below, showing that the built-up area had shifted steadily westwards either because of the growth of the town or owing to the gradual encroachment of the river;

while the upper levels were quite extensive each as we went down diminished in extent until of Level X only a narrow strip was found along the limit of our excavation, breaking away where the steep cliff fell to the old river bed. The earliest level dated only to the eighth century B.C., so that between it and the time of the destruction of Alalakh there was a gap of 400 years, nor was there anything to link up the harbour with Alalakh during the time of its prosperity.

This breach in historical continuity was disconcerting. I was morally certain that the harbour had always served the city and even when the latter was wiped out must have been quickly reorganized for the purposes of international trade, but a moral certainty is a poor basis for history. It would be difficult to dispute my thesis that the greater part of the ancient mound had been washed away, but for the further hypothesis that it had contained building strata going back in time for 2000 years there was really no evidence at all, nor any possibility of finding any on the spot. Fortunately the proof of the theory was ultimately forthcoming, though in a manner as unexpected as it was interesting.

We found that in all the ten levels, ranging in date from the eighth to the fourth centuries B.C., the buildings were very much alike. The walls were of mud brick laid, almost always, upon stone foundations which sometimes were carried up above floor level to form what was really a damp-course; they were fairly heavy walls, averaging about two feet in thickness, but there was no reason to suspect that any of the buildings were of more than one storey — certainly there was nowhere a sign of a staircase. The floors were of beaten clay or mud, in the lower levels laid over a bed of pebbles – this because of the damp; in the higher levels, in which the buildings stood well above the surrounding plain, pebbles were not necessary and were not used. There were no roofing-tiles, and roofs must have been like those of Moslem houses of the present day, nearly flat, composed of layers of matting, reeds, and mud laid over closely-set poplar poles. The buildings form blocks or *insulae* which are approximately rectangular and reasonably uniform in size; between these are streets or lanes intersecting at right angles, gravel-paved, often with a drain along the middle whose cover of stone slabs forms a pavement; there are slight irregularities which must be due to the accidents of owners' rights on either side of the

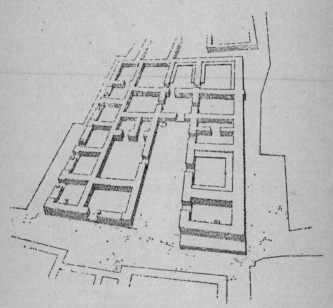

Fig. 26 (a). *Al Mina warehouses: plan*

thoroughfare, but these are reduced to a minimum. In the *insulae* one can recognize not indeed uniformity but something at least approaching a standard plan. A wide doorway from the street leads into a courtyard with a range of storerooms along either side, a large one in the centre and smaller ones at the ends, and four more or less square rooms at the back; there may be a very small isolated building in the courtyard. This is the main building of the block; the remaining space is taken up by a row, or rows, along the street, of small rooms having no connexion with that building or with each other.

Had this been a residential town we should, on the evi-

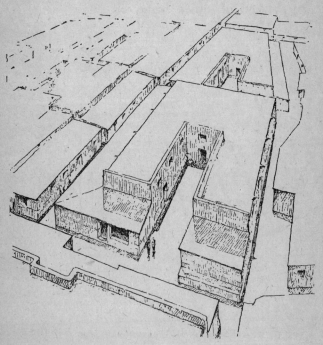

Fig. 26 (b). *Al Mina warehouses: restoration*

dence of the buildings, have judged it to have been poor, if not barbarous; mere huts of mud-brick, one storey high, with mud-plastered walls and with no pretence to decoration or to architectural style, would seem to call for no more flattering description. But it was not a residential town, and the buildings, which would have been poor as private houses, were perfectly adequate to their purpose; what we

have here are the business premises of merchants engaged
in the import and export trade between Asia and the Aegean.

This is made quite clear by the contents of the buildings,
especially in the upper levels where things were better
preserved. Thus in a single building of Level III which had
been burnt, so that objects had been left *in situ* and the
furnishing of many of the rooms was virtually intact, we
could see that the whole of it was given over to goods, and
these were stored in separate categories, a magazine-room
being devoted to each class; one room was filled with great
wine-jars, another with small oil-bottles of local make, a
third with imported Greek unguent-pots, a fourth with big
bell-shaped mixing-bowls, and so on. Each of the large
buildings in an *insula* was the business office of one firm; in
the go-downs were stored the Asiatic goods ready for export,
and the goods disembarked from incoming merchantmen
were warehoused here for eventual sale to the land-traders
whose caravans would transport them to the cities of the
interior. The isolated room in the court was probably the
office of the tally-clerk. The small disconnected rooms along
the street frontage were shops of the 'lock-up' type belonging to retail traders dealing with the local market, or they
were workshops; one, in which we found a number of
small bars of silver and various pieces of jewellery, must
have been the premises of a working goldsmith. In a few,
a very few, cases the presence of a grave under the floor of
a building showed that a merchant might live in his business
premises, for while we have plenty of analogies for the
burying of the dead under the houses in which they had
lived it is scarcely conceivable that the custom should arise
of burial under a business office or warehouse. But apart
from these few burials all the evidence is against the
buildings having been used for residential purposes, and
we have to conclude that the majority of the tradesmen
lived elsewhere. The port cannot have been a salubrious
spot. It lay very low, on ground which was liable to be
flooded (as indeed was proved by our finding masses of

sand and silt above the ruins of the lower-lying buildings of Level IV), and most of the ground round about must have been marsh scarcely redeemed from the sea; the warehouses had to be at the harbour, but no one would live there if he could help it.

Tales of various discoveries that had been made in the past drew our attention to a little hill close to the river and about three miles inland from the harbour. It was a natural hill, a rocky outcrop with a precipitous face on three sides and a gentler sloped approach from the NW., and it was littered with potsherds. A few trial trenches sunk on and below the hill – Sabouni, as it is called – together with surface finds, gave us precisely the results we hoped for. The pottery proved that it had been inhabited during all the periods represented by the ten levels of the harbour, al Mina, and the evidence carried us back far beyond that. There were Mycenaean sherds dating to the thirteenth and twelfth centuries B.C., White Slip 'milk-bowls' of the fifteenth century, and a cylinder seal of about the eighteenth. The hill-top had been fortified with a massive enceinte wall of rubble and brick – that was the acropolis – and there had been other buildings on the flat ground at its foot. It is fairly certain that this was the place where lived the merchants who did business at al Mina. Others, very likely, had villas elsewhere, on the rising ground where stands the little modern town of Sueidia – at least, we found on two sites there potsherds of the classical Greek period; but Sabouni was the town proper, standing to al Mina much in the relation of Athens to the Peiraeus. Of course at al Mina there were some residents of the poorer sort, storekeepers, dock labourers, sailors and fishermen and petty traders tied down to their work, but the richer merchants lived in the healthy surroundings of Sabouni and came down to their offices every morning.

The evidence that the harbour really was in use from early times justifies what has been said in previous chapters of this book about the export trade of Alalakh; but the great interest of the excavations at al Mina lay in the fact that they carried on the history of the trade from the point where it broke off with the destruction of the inland capital.

The late Mycenaean pottery which we found at Sabouni (though not at al Mina, since it would have been only in that part of the mound which has disappeared) gave us a curious link with tradition.

Herodotus states that the Greek hero Amphilochus, who must have lived about the time of the siege of Troy since he was the son of Amphiaraüs, one of the Seven who fought against Thebes, built the city of Posideïum on the Syrian coast; the city was flourishing in the fifth century B.C. From the geographical references found in later Greek writers it is certain that Posideïum must be identified with our port of al Mina *plus* the hill town of Sabouni related with it. That the legend of Amphilochus is founded on fact seems to be shown by discoveries made by Turkish archaeologists in Cilicia, where references have been found to another Greek hero who was associated with Amphilochus, and it is noteworthy too that a mythological legend current in classical Greece has for its scene Mount Kasios, which rises at the mouth of the Orontes, and the Greeks must have got the story (of which an Asiatic text has been found) from al Mina at a very early date. If al Mina was destroyed by the People of the Sea, which we can safely assume to have been the case, and was refounded soon afterwards, chiefly to serve the Greek trade, then Herodotus' story is likely to be literally true.

In the lowest excavated levels, X and IX, very little survived of the buildings but pottery was fairly abundant; much of it was imported and the imported wares all came from the eastern Greek islands, produced between about 750 and 700 B.C. (Pl. 19 b). The disappearance of the old Mycenaean pottery had not interfered with the trade passing through our Syrian harbour; on the contrary, whereas in the old days it had been for the most part limited to Crete and Cyprus, now the ramifications of commerce had ex-

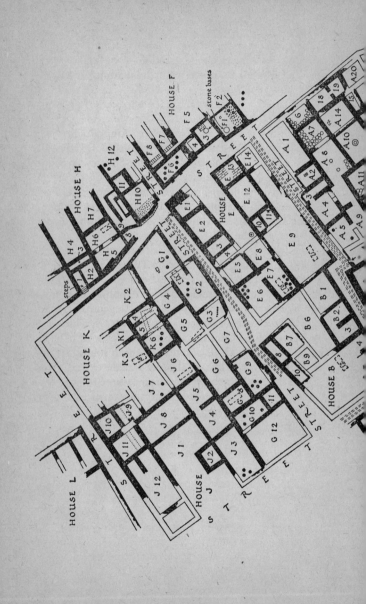

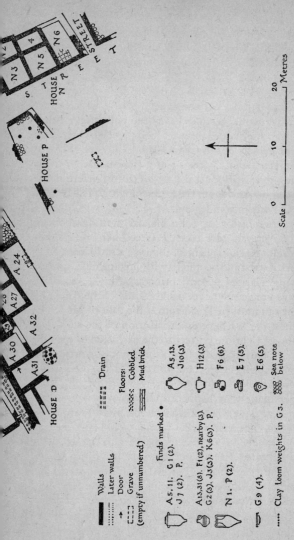

Fig. 27. *The layout of warehouses at al Mina, Level III*, the types concerned being given by the notes in the caption.

The bulk storage of pottery vessels is indicated by massed circles, the types concerned being given by the notes in the caption.

Walls
Later walls
Door
Grave
(empty if unnumbered)

Drain

Floors:
Cobbled
Mud brick

Finds marked •

A5, 11. G1 (2).
J7 (2). P.

A5, 13.
J10 (3).

A13, 31 (8). F1 (2), nearby (3).
G2 (2), J3 (3). K6 (2). P.

H12 (3)

N1. P (2).

F6 (6).

E7 (5).

G9 (4).

E6 (5).

Clay Loom weights in G3.

See note
below

HOUSE D   A31   A32   A27   A30   29

HOUSE P

HOUSE
N6

N3   N5   4

STREET   N6

STREET

A24

Scale   0   10   20   Metres

tended far more widely and there can be recognized the wares of Delos, Rhodes, Tenos, and the Cycladic islands; Posideïum had become an emporium for the manufacturers of Eastern Greece.

In Level VIII a few walls of the previous period are re-used as foundations, but the general plan is quite different and the town would seem to have been built afresh on new lines. The pottery too shows a complete change and is almost exclusively of the Cyprus Iron Age type (Pl. 20 b), either imports from Cyprus or of a local fabric so closely resembling the Cypriote that it is difficult to determine the place of origin. And again the archaeological facts bring us into touch with ancient legends.

A Byzantine historian, John Malalas, writing about the district of Antioch, says that the Greek hero Kasos, after whom Mount Kasios is named, founded a settlement on the north Syrian coast and peopled it with Cretans and Cypriotes, and having married a local princess, Amyke, ruled the territory as king. Amyke means 'the Lady of the Amq', and the settlement must be Posideïum at the foot of Mt Kasios, and in the story we have an explanation of the sudden introduction of Cypriote pottery to the exclusion of the other island wares current heretofore. It was not of course a new settlement on virgin soil, but looking at the very scanty remains of Level IX and the new lay-out of Level VIII we can understand what happened. Kasos was a merchant-adventurer of days when merchant and pirate were almost synonymous. Observing what profits were being made by the island traders out of the commerce with the interior of Asia he collected from Cyprus an armed force of rival merchants and captured and sacked Posideïum, after which he rebuilt it for himself and, having made friends with the people of the Amq so as to secure the interior caravan-routes, enjoyed a monopoly of the port's business. To this extent he was the founder of the settlement. But his monopoly did not last for very long. Judging by the evidence of the ruins Level VIII was short-lived, lasting perhaps from

700 to not much after 675 B.C. when most of the buildings
were in bad state and had to be reconstructed. Level VII
does not show any real break in continuity, the warehouses
being but new versions of the old at a slightly higher level.
But in the pottery the Cypriote tradition, while still preva-
lent, is none the less losing ground; there is a recrudescence
of the sub-geometric island wares and in particular of that
of Rhodes, and by the end of the period (which again was
but a short one) the Rhodian and the Cypriote wares were
pretty fairly balanced; in face of the vastly superior pottery
obtainable from Rhodes Cyprus was being driven off the
market.

This is very clear in the light of Levels VI and V. In the
former there was a lot of rebuilding on new lines, the old
Level VII magazines having fallen hopelessly into decay,
whereas the Level V buildings are but those of Level VI
repaired and refloored. In the former there is still a certain
amount of Cypriote pottery, in the latter it has disappeared
altogether. This does not mean that all commercial relations
with Cyprus had come to an end; Cypriote terra-cottas and
limestone sculpture carry on the tradition into Level IV;
but as regards pottery other Greek centres were producing
wares more suited to the luxury trade passing through the
harbour of Posideïum; the import-merchants patronized
the best centres of manufacture and demanded from them
the best quality of goods made there. The result is that here,
in an Asiatic port, we found a collection of early Greek
pottery as wide in range and as fine in quality as has come
from any site in Greece itself. It must be remembered that
the magazines at al Mina were merely for the storage of
goods in transit; what we found were the bits of vases
broken in packing or unpacking, and even so most of the
fragments would have been swept away, leaving only such
as were overlooked and trodden into the mud floors; of
the goods that passed through safely we have no evidence
at all. Sometimes, where a magazine had caught fire and its
contents had perished, we had better luck, for generally a

new floor would be laid over the debris and the proportion of pottery would be vastly greater and complete vessels might be recovered, but for the most part we have only the accidental survivals of accidents. In spite of this, the fragments from Levels VI and V are extraordinarily varied and informative (Pl. 20 a). We can see that the main centre on which Posideïum drew was again Rhodes, whose delicate egg-shell-thin cups and jugs of lustrous black with bands of purple, red, and white obviously appealed to the Asiatic customer, for the fragments of them are particularly numerous, and the Rhodian 'orientalizing' wares show how much the Greek potter was influenced by the eastern trade. In Level VI there was a fair amount of Proto-Corinthian pottery but in Level V the early Corinthian was much less common. The plain black ware of Lesbos was favoured by one or two dealers and one seems to have specialized in Chiote or Naukratite vases, while from various islands came the charming little cups decorated with painted figures of birds which are in direct descent from the Geometric style.

The Level V pottery takes us down to about 550 B.C. and then there is in our series a gap of some thirty years for which we have only a single sherd. This may mean that for a time the operations of the port were suspended by political conditions, but against that we must set the fact that Greek pottery of that period is found both at Sabouni and elsewhere in northern Syria, so that imports were coming in, and Posideïum is the natural channel for them. I think that the more likely explanation is that before the Level IV buildings were put up an unusually clean sweep was made of the site which destroyed the evidence that would otherwise have existed for the business activities of the later part of Level V. There certainly was just such a clean sweep. Level IV is laid out in *insulae* which do not correspond to those of Level V, and generally below the floors we found a layer of rubbish separating them from the stumps of the Level V walls, and this implies a regular process of demolition which might well account for the disappearance of a whole stratum of potsherds. The rebuilding and re-planning of the warehouses coincides with (and may result from) a revolution in the import business. From that moment, which we can date to about the year 520 B.C., every imported vase found in the harbour site comes from Athens (Pl. 21 a). There were statuettes from Cyprus, blue-glazed scarabs from Naukratis in Egypt, vessels of polychrome 'Phoenician' glass probably from southern Syria, but in the pottery line Athens enjoyed a complete monopoly. As in previous periods so now goods of the highest quality were being imported, presumably for the use of Persian court circles which would naturally demand the best (Pl. 21 b). Many of the fragments found can be assigned to individual painters whose works are known, and some of them are peculiarly fine; but side by side with these we find wares evidently intended for a more general and a cheaper market. The most interesting point about these, which throws a new light on Attic vase-making, is the constant repetition of the same design. Thus in one room of Level III we found, more or less well preserved, upwards of ten little unguent-vases all painted, rather roughly, with a woman's head and a flower (Pl. 22 a) and half a dozen examples of a similar vase decorated with an acanthus design, all exactly alike. Since the broken vessels that we find are but a small percentage of those imported, these unguent-vases must represent a very large consignment of each type. Whether these duplicate vases were all painted in succession by one craftsman or whether a single one designed by a good artist was set up and copied by a number of less skilled slaves working as a team, in either case we have here proof of a system of mass-production in the *ateliers* of Athens which we had not hitherto suspected; it is a new sidelight on Attic trade. Another point of interest was the finding of fragments of three of the big 'Panathenaic' vases which were formerly supposed to have been used exclusively as prizes given to the victors in the great Panathenaic games; that they were on sale in Poseïdeum shows that they might be bought by anyone as souvenirs and even exported. One of them had been broken and riveted in antiquity and was found by us in a quarter of the town which, judging by the number of mended vases there, contained the second-hand bazaar; but the two others were probably new when they were accidentally broken in the warehouse.

Level IV lasted from 520 to 430 B.C. The really surprising thing is that at that date it should have existed at all. The Athenian merchants secured the monopoly of trade with the East just about the time when the conquests of Cyrus in Ionia were beginning to establish Persia as the enemy of Greece. In 490 B.C. came the first invasion of Greece and the battle of Marathon, ten years later the great invasion led by Xerxes; Athens was captured, and immediately afterwards the Persians were defeated in the battles of Salamis and Plataea; the invaders were driven out of Greece, but the war continued, and for nearly a century there was intermittent fighting between Athenians and Persians. But all the time when Athens was at death-grips with Persia, warring desperately by land and by sea, Athenian merchant-ships were casting anchor by the wharves of Poseïdeum, a Persian port in the Fifth Satrapy of the Persian Empire, and trading peacefully with the enemy; it is a curious witness to the importance which Athens attached to her overseas trade that even when war might well have usurped all her energies 'business' had to be carried on 'as usual'. Nor is it a less striking commentary on the methods of Persian government which would not only allow the Satrap or Governor of one of its great provinces to continue in war-time its normal trade with the enemy but would countenance the presence on Persian soil of an Athenian merchant colony – for it is certain that many of the dealers there were Greeks – and in its encouragement of commerce would go even further; we found great quantities of coins in the ruins, and all those of smaller denominations were what one would expect to find in a Persian port on the Mediterranean,

Persian coins struck in the mints of Sidon, Arvad, and Cyprus; but the larger coins were without exception Attic, silver tetradrachms either struck in Athens or locally made in imitation of the Athenian. For local purchases then and for retail trade with the Phoenician coast Persian money was used; but for wholesale transactions the regular currency of the port was that of the enemy with which Persia was at war.

By 430 B.C. the warehouses had done their term of service and had to be renewed; Level III is simply a reconstruction of Level IV. But in the year 375 B.C. or thereabouts there was a disastrous fire which destroyed most of the buildings and the new magazines that rose in their place were on the same lines (generally using as foundations the stumps of the old walls) but with floors separated from those of the former period by as much as three feet of burnt rubbish. In consequence, Level III is particularly well preserved, and in most of the stores we were able to compare in detail the contents and uses of the different rooms in each; everything was classified, and it was seldom that remains of vessels of different sorts were found together – even the lamp-fillers would be, not with the lamps, but in the next room. The wide assortment of weights – Greek, Syrian, Mesopotamian – bore witness to the international character of the business done; metal-work was coming from as far afield as Lake Van in the Caucasus; Syria or Egypt was contributing amulets of polychrome glass in the form of grotesque human heads; and the quicksilver (used by goldsmiths) which we found loose in the soil probably came from the Almaden mines of Spain. The port flourished exceedingly. When in 333 B.C. Alexander the Great overthrew the Persian Empire and Posideïum became in name as well as in fact a Greek town, when a single government extending over the whole of the eastern Mediterranean and western Asia assured even freer trade than before and in the cash-boxes of the Posideïum merchants the world-wide currency of Macedon replaced the old coins of Athens, the citizens must surely have believed that a new era of prosperity had dawned. It was perhaps in that belief that they set up in the local temple a marble statue of the City Goddess carved in the style favoured by Alexander and his successors; we found the battered head, which had once worn a battlemented crown of gilt bronze or of gold, cast away in the town ruins (Pl. 22 b).

That head, a few coins of the followers of Alexander, and a single clay vase were all that we found to testify to the existence of the place after Alexander's death. In 301 B.C. Seleucus founded, four miles north of al Mina, his new harbour of Seleucia with its great artificial basins and splendid buildings. Faced by such rivalry the old port simply ceased to exist – indeed, it is likely that Seleucus forcibly removed its people to his new foundation. It had already suffered very severely when in 413 B.C. Ptolemy of Egypt captured and sacked it – that may account for the smashing of the statue of the City Goddess – and now, instead of being rebuilt once more, it was deserted altogether. For nearly nine hundred years it had outlived Alalakh, the city it had been built to serve; it had carried on its trade for the Syro-Hittite kinglets and it had been the commercial outlet of the Persian Empire. Now the flamboyant Seleucid capital, Antioch on the Orontes, required a modern harbour to replace the riverside wharves of ancient Posideïum, and even if a few fishing-boats continued to tie up against the river bank, as they do to this day, it was against reason to hope that the ruin-mound in the marshes could ever again rank as a port for overseas shipping.

Epilogue

Port St Symeon

*

FOR 400 years then the site of Posideïum was deserted and its name passed out of memory. When, in the first century A.D., the Romans dredged the lower course of the Orontes and made it navigable for small craft as far inland as Antioch a few buildings, customs sheds or what not, would naturally spring up at the river's mouth, and by the fourth century may have developed into a little shipping station, for two late classical writers mention a natural harbour close to Seleucia called Bytyllion, which cannot have been other than our al Mina. Actually we did find remains of buildings which we could assign to the fifth or sixth century, and one at least of them had been a building of some importance, for it had a stone screen and arcade with elaborately moulded column-bases; one of the stone shafts had carved on it a double cross reminding one that Antioch was now one of the chief centres of Christianity; moreover the coins found here, coins of the emperors Justin, Justinian, and Heraclius, witnessed to the fact that in and after the sixth century the old harbour was alive again. This was indeed natural. In A.D. 526 a great earthquake ruined Seleucia, and further shocks in the course of the century completed the destruction of Seleucia and of Antioch alike; the latter recovered to some degree, but the vast artificial works of the former could not be restored in a degenerate age; the impoverished citizens of a smaller Antioch, cut off from the sea because, owing to the earthquake, the Orontes was no longer navigable, had no alternative but to use the old anchorage at its mouth. But the decay of Antioch and the falling-off of its trade spelled a short life for Bytyllion; our excavations produced nothing that could be dated to the later seventh and eighth centuries. But from the middle of the ninth century onwards the material which we brought to light was abundant; there were remains of buildings, some of them on a considerable scale, and there were masses of pottery, much of it plain, but much of it painted and glazed; some was almost certainly of local fabric, but there were many examples of glazed pottery, including lustre-ware, which had come from Mesopotamia and evidently was meant for export abroad, passing through al Mina in transit. Once again the port was playing the same part as it had played 2000 years before, but now it was the Abbaside Caliphs of Baghdad and Samarra who were trading with the western world of the Mediterranean. Until the Byzantine invasion of A.D. 969 al Mina prospered; after that time it suffered a fresh eclipse, for with Antioch in Byzantine hands the trade with Mesopotamia was cut off and the Byzantines had nothing to export; we found only eighteen coins to represent the passing of the next 130 years.

But in 1097 the Christian warriors of the First Crusade besieged and eventually took Antioch and in the same year the Genoese fleet captured al Mina. This meant a new era of prosperity, and after 1188, when Saladin conquered and held Latakia further down the Syrian coast, the only harbour still in the hands of the Dukes of Antioch became really important. On the rising ground a mile inland rose the residential town of Suwaidiya, but the harbour also rapidly increased in size and far beyond the limits of our excavation one can trace the massive concrete walls, the quays, and the outlines of buildings constructed in fine cut stone. It was now known as the Port of St Symeon, so called after the second of those curious ascetics who gained, or exhibited, their sanctity by spending their lives aloft on the top of a high pillar – his monastery and tomb crown a neighbouring hill. The coins that we found start soon after the Crusaders' victory with those of Tancred, who became Duke in 1104,[1] but such early pieces are very few in number and the bulk come after the loss of Latakia; it is to this later period that we must assign the main buildings and at least the majority of the objects found in the ruins. By far the most interesting discovery was concerned with the pottery used by the Crusaders.[2] This was a brownish ware covered with a white slip through which designs were cut into the brown clay before firing; then colour was added, green and yellow and sometimes purple, and the whole was coated with a lead glaze which in the furnace took on a yellowish tint (Pl. 23). The presence of a few 'kiln-wasters' proved that the vessels were made on the spot, in the Port of St Symeon itself. Examples of this coarse but gay glazed earthenware have been found in other places in Syria, as far south as Mt Carmel, but the export went much farther afield than that; a fine bowl now in the Victoria and Albert Museum was built as an ornament into the tower of a church in Pisa! Really it is a very decorative ware. The designs are usually simple and the drawing crude – the craftsmen employed were native Syrians, as is shown by an Arabic inscription on one piece and by the oriental character of many of the patterns, and Christian motives are rare, though we have one big fragment with an elaborate representation of a Crusader in chain armour (Pl. 23, No. 4); but the splashes of colour on the white ground are skilfully applied and the general effect is most pleasing. The Crusaders themselves must have taken home specimens of their household pottery, and since Port St Symeon was making it between 1200 and 1268 when Antioch and its harbour were captured by the Mamelukes, long before any such wares were manufactured in Italy, it may well be that vessels so much admired served as models for Italian potters and that Italian maiolica was in part at least inspired by the products of al Mina.

1. See E. S. G. Robinson and D. Allen, *Numismatic Chronicle*, 5th Series, vol. XVII, 1937.

2. *v.* Arthur Lane, 'Medieval Finds at al Mina in North Syria', *Archaeologia*, vol. LXXXVII, 1938, p. 19.

We began our excavations there in the hope of finding the channel through which the influences of Asiatic art were brought to bear on the western world of the Mediterranean. Discoveries at Atchana proved that this was true of the place at least as far back in time as the eighteenth century B.C. when Crete learnt from Asia the techniques of architecture and of painting in fresco. Unexpectedly, the remains at al Mina gave us not only relations with the Greek islands during the eighth and later centuries, but also the trading links between Athens and Persia which held fast throughout the agony of the Persian War. It is curiously fitting that the tradition should be maintained to the end and that when Posideïum revived for a brief spell as Port St Symeon it should still furnish to the craftsmen of the western world oriental ideas and techniques to inspire new arts in Europe.

After its capture by Baibars the Mameluke the port was deserted indeed and its buildings crumbled until in course of time the flattened stone-strewn ground was turned to ploughland. Sailing-boats still bring cargoes of timber or cement to the river mouth, but the mud-brick custom sheds scarcely deserve the title of 'al Mina', The Harbour. The old names have passed out of memory and the Alaouite saint, Sheikh Yusuf, has usurped all that is left of St Symeon's Port. Yet where so much has been forgotten it is possible that one tradition survives. A mile or so away to the north there stands on the edge of the lonely beach of black sand a solid whitewashed dome (Pl. 24 b) revered alike by Alaouites, Moslems, and Christians who from all the district round come on pilgrimage to burn incense at the common shrine; if you ask them who is the saint so honoured they will tell you 'it is the Sheikh al Bahr', 'the Lord of the Sea', and they will tell you nothing more. I like to think that the old sea-god whom the sailors of Alalakh knew 4000 years ago, whom the Greeks, when they came, identified with their own Poseidon and named the port of their founding Posideïum after him, is still, as the Sheikh al Bahr, ignorantly worshipped.

Chronology Tables
and Index

COMPARATIVE CHRONOLOGY

DATE	ATCHANA LEVEL	MESOPOTAMIA	EGYPT	NORTH SYRIA
	Tell esh Sheikh	Tell Halaf al 'Ubaid		
3400 (?)	Tabara al Akrad	Uruk		
3400–3300	Level XVII		Middle Pre-dynastic	
3300–3200	Level XVI			
3200–3100	Level XV			Carchemish, Late Chalcolithic
3100–2900	Level XIV	Jamdet Nasr		Carchemish, First Bronze
2900–2700	Level XIII	Early Dynastic (Ur Royal Tombs)		
2700–2350	Level XII	Early Dynastic		
2350–2200	Level XI	Sargon of Akkad Naram-Sin		
2200–2050	Level X	Guti		
2050–1900	Level IX	3rd Dynasty of Ur; latest Kul-tepe colony		
1900–1780	Level VIII		XIIth Dynasty conquest of N. Syria	
1780–1750	Level VII Abban Hammurabi Yarim-Lim Niqme-epukh	Hammurabi of Babylon Rim-Sin of Larsa		
1750–1595	Level VI			Cypriote red-on-black pottery Mursilis the Hit-tite captures Aleppo, 1595
1595–1447	Level V Phase A: 1595–1527		Thothmes I's campaign to Euphrates 1527	Rise of the Mitanni
	Phase B: 1527–1447 Tahu made king of Nuh-assi		Thotmes III takes tribute of Alalakh 1483	
1447–1370	Level IV Niqmepa Ilim-ilimma Idri-mi Adad-nirari Takuwa		Amenhetep II, 1447 Thothmes IV (treaty with Mitanni 1420) Amenhetep III Akhenaten 1375	*Mitanni* Shaushshatar Artatama Dushratta *Hittites* Subbiluliuma *c.* 1387 defeats Dushratta 1370 Mycenaeans con-quer Crete
1370–1347	Level III			Subbiluliuma dies 1347
1347–*c.* 1283	Level		Ramses II (bat-tle of Kadesh 1289)	Mursilis II
1283–1194	Level I Phase A: 1283–1241	Shalmaneser I of Assyria Tukulti-Inurta (takes Babylon, 1241)	Ramses makes peace with Hattusilis (1273)	Muwatallis Hattusilis Tudkhalia IV (1250)
	Phase B: 1241–1194			
1194	The invasion of the Peoples of the Sea and the destruction of Alalakh			

CHRONOLOGY OF AL MINA

B.C.

Before 1200	Evidence from Sabouni only	
After 1194	Re-founding of the port (Posideïum) by Amphilochus	Evidence from Sabouni only
750–700	Trade with various Greek islands	Levels X–IX
700–675	Conquest and resettlement by Kasos and his Cypriotes	Level VIII
675–550	Trade with Rhodes, Corinth, and the Greek islands	Levels VII–V
520–301	Athens has the monopoly of the trade with Persia	Levels IV–III
301	Founding of Seleucia and ruin of Posideïum	

A.D.

400–500	Re-founding of the port (Bytyllion)	Level I
526–650	Destruction of Seleucia and rise of Bytyllion; decay after 650	
850–969	al Mina under the Abbaside Caliphs	Level I B
969–1097	Decay under the Byzantines	
1097–1286	The Crusaders' Port of St Symeon	Level I A
1286	Capture of Antioch by the Mamelukes; the end of Port St Symeon	

Index